The Church that Dares to Change

The Church that Dares to Change

A selection of summary of sermons from over 600 delivered from the pulpit of Circular Road Baptist Chapel and elsewhere during my pastoral ministry of 11 years and 3 months.

(April 1991 to June 2002)

M.K. Pramanik

ISPCK
2006

The Church that Dares to Change—Published by the Rev. Dr. Ashish Amos of the Indian Society for Promoting Christian Knowledge (ISPCK), Post Box 1585, Kashmere Gate, Delhi-110006.

© Author, 2006

All rights reserved. No part of this book may be reproduced or transmitted in any form or by any means, electronic, mechanical, photocopying, recording, or by any information storage and retrieval system, without the prior permission in writing from the publisher.

The views expressed in the book are that of the author and the publisher takes no responsibility of any of the statements.

ISBN: 81-7214-939-5

Cover design : Author

Laser typeset by
ISPCK, Post Box 1585, 1654 Madarsa Road, Kashmere Gate, Delhi-110006 • *Tel:* 23866323, *Fax:* 91-11-23865490.
e-mail: ashish@ispck.org.in • mail@ispck.org.in
website: www.ispck.org.in

This book is affectionately dedicated to my beloved wife Putul, and daughter Madhusmita for their constant encouragement, suggestions and help in preparation of this book.

Contents

Dedication	v
Foreword 1	ix
Foreword 2	xiii
Preface	xv

Chapter 1	**My Testimony**	1
	1.1 How I became a Pastor?	1
	1.2 Why I took retirement?	10
Chapter 2	**A note from the author**	16
Chapter 3	**"Lord, make me your own"** **(Redeemed or regenerated life)**	20
	3.1 Living faith	20
	3.2 Sufferings and trials of faith	32
Chapter 4	**"Lord, draw me closer to you"** **(Devotional or surrendered life)**	38
	4.1 Worshipful life	38
	4.2 Prayer life	46
	4.3 Reading the Word of God	54
	4.4 Church life	56
	4.4.1 Baptism	63
	4.4.2 Lord's Supper	64
	4.4.3 Revival	67
	4.4.4 Offerings and Tithes	73

Chapter 5	**"Lord, equip me to bear fruit"** **(Service in God's Kingdom on earth)**	**75**
	5.1 Discipleship	75
	5.2 Fellowship	85
	5.3 Mission and Evangelism	89
Chapter 6	**"Lord, make my life a miracle"** **(Sanctified life or holiness in life)**	**104**
	6.1 Christian maturity – life in all its fullness	104
Chapter 7	**"Lord, help me to proclaim Jesus as the Lord in all celebrations"**	**118**
	7.1 Christmas	118
	7.2 New Year	125
	7.3 Palm Sunday	131
	7.4 Good Friday	135
	7.5 Easter	140
	7.6 Harvest thanksgiving	142
	7.7 Wedding	143
	About the Author	146

Foreword 1

Barbara Ward, the one time Professor of International Economic Development in Columbia University, wrote a penetrating article entitled: 'What can we say that will make us listen?' She assessed the world of her times and concluded that they did not have time anymore to sit in their absolute positions without communication with one another. This spaceship called earth is running out of energy. She stresses that whereas a 'highly dogmatic version of economic and social history' prevents positive dialogue between communities and societies, '**the Christian Churches** have started a series of encounters and types of common action – social and international affairs – that concentrate on the points of agreement and common direction'.

This dynamism is part of the content of the subject of this book by Rev. Dr. M.K. Pramanik.

Working for many years in the steel industry of India as a top level executive, he responded to the compelling call of Jesus of Nazareth to follow Him to submit the rule of God and turn away from ideologies and personal opinion. The consent he gave to this call is what makes the difference with those who would 'merely follow because they are interested' and those whom Jesus has chosen and called. This constitutes the beginning of the 'I-Thou' dialogical relationship which is center of discipleship. Discipleship has consequence. This 'called' and the 'chosen' are never an end in themselves, they are 'appointed' to be productive: fishermen become 'fishers of men'.

The core of biblical history is the story of the calling of a visible community of humankind to be God's people.

Persons who are called to constitute a visible community. The visible fellowship that results and exists to carry out God's will in this world. God's will in this world is that all 'be saved and come to the knowledge of the truth (1 Timothy 2: 4). Some form of structure is essential for the functioning of this community. But the essence is not the 'structure' but the community. The community's task is to obey Jesus Christ, who will achieve God's purpose in the world with them and through them. This obedience is expressed corporately and individually, but never outside the consciousness of the community. The structure of the community is only for the achievement of this purpose. When Dr. Pramanik talks about 'The Church that dares to change' he is speaking about this community.

It is different from all other human communities because it is God's new humanity. The glue that holds them together is the hearing, believing and obeying the 'good news', and not merely racial, national, class, cultural or linguistic ties. The community finds its continuity by participating in the sacraments. The dynamics of the community is the receiving and abiding in the Holy Spirit. This community is 'the community of God'. The descriptive term is 'community', but the operative word is 'God or Christ'.

Over the years, when Dr. Pramanik was a pastor of the Lower Circular Baptist Church, Calcutta, these sermons were preached by him. He preached these messages to the congregations with the intended call for them to change and be 'the community of God' in that great city.

Through the effective communication of the Word of God, human community dared to change to be an instrument in God's hand to influence the other human communities along with the Lower Circular Baptist Church. The truth set them free to act and to be the people of God within the great city.

The truth sets the ordinary human communities free from the bondage that prevents them from experiencing the 'freedom' of what they can be and become.

C.S. Lewis thought that 'Where God gives the gift, the 'foolishness of preaching' (1 Cor. 1:21) is till mighty. But best of all is a team of two; one to deliver the preliminary intellectual barrage, and the other to follow up with a direct attack on the heart.' The preaching of Dr. Pramanik had the intellectual as well as the emotional appeal to the heart.

As a congregation with a big heart, the Lower Circular Road Baptist Church still exists and exerts her influence. Dr. Pramanik has shepherded them further into the obedience of God. This book will recall the days when he learned by serving the people of God and will help those who want to find 'dare to change' based on the Word of God.

Noah's ark is often to describe the congregation with some poetic humor. William Warburton, Bishop of Gloucester, in a letter to a friend written on June 13, 1751 wrote, **"The church, like the Ark of Noah, is worth saving, not for the sake of the unclean beasts and vermin that almost filled it, and probably made most noise and clamor in it, but for the little corner of rationality that was as much distressed by the stink within and the tempest without."**

Do read the book. Learn what makes "the church that dares to change" from the one who was sent out to serve the 'community of God'.

Rev. Dr. Samuel Kamaleson
Vice President (at large)
World Vision International, CA, USA

Foreword - 2

I have known Rev. Dr. M.K. Pramanik for over two decades now, a very warm personality, a committed Christian pastor and a very reliable friend. Mrs. Pramanik is an equally warm personality – both of them together are committed to pastoral ministry of the Baptist Church.

Dr. Pramanik is a firm believer in Jesus Christ and is committed to the Word of God in his ministry as well as in his daily life. I had always been amazed and admired the decision of both Dr. and Mrs. Pramanik in giving up a prosperous executive position in the Steel Authority of India only to take up a humble position of a pastor of Baptist Church in Calcutta, at a time and place where he enjoyed high reputation in his secular job. The commitment of this family to their faith and their decision, to give priority to full time service of the church as a pastor, has no parallel in my knowledge of the life of the church in India.

Personally, he has been a pillar of strength to me in my work as Master of the Serampore College Council, of which he has been a valued member and also Vice-Master for a period. His own commitment to values – Christian values of integrity and efficiency made him extend whole hearted support to my struggle to establish integrity and efficiency in our immediate and extended responsibilities of the Serampore College Council.

No wonder, with this background of faith, his ministry and his sermons during his pastoral services at the Lower Circular Road Baptist Church, published in the following pages only reflect his deep faith in Jesus Christ, his integrity in his relation with the parishioners and a source of inspiration to the believers and worshippers at his church.

He is very much desired in many other ministries like World Vision of India and the Baptist Church of USA.

I am glad he has decided to publish some of his inspiring sermons. Infact, I encouraged him to do so.

With great joy, I commend these sermons to all Christians.

Dr. K. Rajaratnam
Master, Serampore College Council

Preface

In the second year of my pastoral ministry in 1993, the Spirit of God laid on my heart two tasks to be accomplished – the first, before I take retirement from the church and the second after I retire.

The first task was to plant a church for the Bengali speaking people (Bengali is the state language of West Bengal) in a new area but within the city of Calcutta. The second task was to compile and publish a book containing summary of selected sermons from all sermons delivered from the pulpit of the Circular Road Baptist Chapel and elsewhere during my ministry in the church.

The church at Circular Road is the second Baptist Church established by seven like minded missionaries of Baptist Missionary Society (BMS) working under the leadership and guidance of Rev. Dr. William Carey, the first BMS missionary to India. He is known as the "father of modern missionary movement". When this church was established in 1818, Dr. Carey had shifted to Serampore but was available to serve this church as its pastor whenever there was need. He also presided over the deacon's meetings and led the Holy Communion several times in church.

I must hasten to add that the deacons and the congregation accepted me as their pastor very lovingly and willingly. This was a great decision since I had no theology degree and my background was different to qualify for becoming a pastor of a heritage and historical mainline church.

I acknowledge with deep gratitude to my pastor late Rev. Dr. Chetti Devashayam for becoming his successor. He got the vision to challenge me to be his successor. He was a loving and a caring pastor, excellent in expository sermons, a man of great international repute being the Professor and Registrar of Serampore Theological University; and as an international speaker in Pastors' Conferences organized by World Vision International, Monrovia, California. Apart from him, I acknowledge many other reputed and great servants of God who have nurtured me in shaping my life and ministry with their teachings. By the grace of God, I was found suitable for taking over the pastoral responsibilities of the Circular Road Baptist Chapel.

Those who have influenced my growth in spiritual life are *Rev. Subodh Sahu, Rev. Dr. Samuel Kamaleson, Rev. Dr. Theodore Williams, Rev. Zac Poonen, Brother Paul Sudhakar and Brother Bhakt Singh*. The last two have gone home to be with the Lord.

The first task of planting church with new Bengali converts in a new area appeared to me an impossible task in the beginning. The church I ministered consisted of English speaking members only. Besides, this is a heritage church with more than 175 years of history and traditions. The church had a definite background for evangelization. I was the second Indian pastor and Bengali speaking worshippers were few. Despite this, my self and my wife started praying, challenging God to make this impossible task possible. We also requested the deacons and the congregation to pray seeking God's ways and means to start this project.

The vision of planting a church for Bengali speaking congregation was accomplished in south Calcutta during my pastoral ministry. God made this possible for His own glory and proved that "with men what is impossible is possible with God".

Preface

The second task is being fulfilled now in publishing this book. I realize with strong conviction I have succeeded in both the tasks given to me when I started my pastoral ministry and it is not for my ability but for God's enabling grace and mercy. It is not me and my wife alone who have been blessed in fulfilling both the tasks, it is also the deacons and the congregation who have prayed with us and have played an important role, particularly in the church planting project.

I do realize that even though I am an unworthy vessel, God made me worthy in pastoral ministry to serve His church for eleven years and three months. I cherish this fulfilling experience. I will, therefore, request you to read my testimony – How I became a pastor and why I took voluntary retirement?

I acknowledge my friends who have helped me at various stages in putting together this book - my granddaughter Ruth for her constant nagging to complete this book; Meera Jha, Sarika Jha and Udya Puri who faithfully typed the manuscript.

As you read through the pages of this book may the Lord grant you double portion of His grace to make you a fruitful vine in God's vineyard.

Ashiana's "The Heritage"   **Rev. Dr. Mohit K. Pramanik**
Sector 4 Vaishali-201012   *Former Pastor*
(National Capital Region)   *Circular Road Baptist Chapel*
New Delhi   *Calcutta*
   1 April 2006

Chapter - 1

My Testimony

1.1. How I became a Pastor?

On a Sunday morning after the worship service in April 1988, my pastor Late Rev. Dr. C. Devasahayam asked me and my wife Putul to stay back and meet him in the manse. During these days our two daughters were studying in New Delhi. The elder one Madhusmita (Madhu) was pursuing her postgraduate studies at the Jawaharlal Nehru University and the younger one Deepanweeta (Pinky) was doing her honors in Economics at the Lady Shriram College, New Delhi.

As we were waiting in the manse, the pastor came, he started telling us about how he and his wife Padma were praying for a successor and the Spirit of God had laid in his heart to request me to be his successor. He also stated that whatever was my decision, I should inform him first and no one should know about this. He also suggested that if my response is in affirmative, I should consult our two daughters in Delhi and come back to him.

While returning home by a car both of us were silently pondering over the conversation we just had with the pastor. After some time, I broke the silence and told Putul, "Our pastor is old enough (he was 72+) to cope with all the pastoral work he does. He is also finding it hard to get a suitable successor during last two years. So he is now desperate to find one and perhaps, because I had told him "there is no success without a successor, he has thought of me."

Next morning, I left for Bombay for a business meeting. Then I was the Managing Director in Government of India undertaking dealing with the Secondary Steel Producers who accounted for about 35% of country's steel production. With my previous experience as the Industrial Adviser to the Government, I had serviced this sector for their technological development, procurement of raw materials from overseas and also issued licenses for plant and machinery. I had, to travel quite extensively within in the country and as well as outside the country in order to finalize contracts for imports. I always had a very busy schedule throughout the week and used to return to Calcutta on Saturday to attend the church on Sunday. I had made a practice not to attend to any secular work on Sunday so that I could give more time to both the worship services and attend to church work as a deacon.

One Sunday evening in Sept. 1988, Putul enquired, what I had thought about the pastor's request and whether I was praying about it? I realised that I had forgotten and did not pray about this during last five months. She then said, "I am praying seriously and am waiting to know from you about the request of the pastor." We then decided to pray individually and together about this during our prayer times. We shared with each other how marvelously God has blessed us and our daughters, even when we are unworthy. He has given us more than what we deserved. We acknowledged His grace in our family life. We also recalled how God granted me life after a very serious scooter accident in 1968 when I was in comma for 8 days. Because of prayers of many godly people, God had granted me recovery in a marvellous way. It was a miracle in my life. Thoughts came to both of us that God had a plan in my life to be a pastor for which He did this miracle. This was also followed by thoughts of inadequacy to become a pastor.

This thought was continuously weighing me down, it compelled me to consult my father and take his advice. In Feb. 89, I made an overnight journey to Sambalpur, Orissa on a Friday evening from Calcutta to meet him. On seeing me, my father thought that this was a surprise visit. But I was looking for a quiet time with him to tell the purpose of my visit. After the family worship on Saturday evening, I informed him that our pastor has requested me to succeed him as the pastor of Circular Road Baptist Church for he had decided to retire. He did not respond that evening nor did he say anything on Sunday morning after family worship. I felt my visit had gone waste since I was disappointed without any response or suggestion from him.

As I was preparing to leave for the railway station, he prayed for my safe return home and told me to come next with Putul, Madhu and Pinky for he had not seen them for a long time. (He passed away in May 89 after a brief illness and did not know that I became a pastor.) I now picked up courage to ask him about his reaction to what I had told him Saturday evening. He did not say "Yes" or "No" to the proposal but asked me two questions.

1. "Do you know the responsibilities of a pastor ?"

2. "Are you equipped to be a pastor ?"

I left Sambalpur, thinking all the way about the two questions. Next Sunday after the worship service, I went to the manse and told my pastor that I think I need to know about the responsibilities of a pastor and I am not adequately equipped to become a pastor. The pastor took me to the church vestry and told me, "Mohit, you have been a deacon for several years in this church, you also preach in the Sunday services, you are a leader in many evangelical organizations such as EFI and UESI. You have attended many international conferences- "Asia Pacific Congress on Evangelism" in Singapore in 1968 and Congress on "Let the earth hear His voice" held in Lausanne, Switzerland in 1974. So you have learned the challenges and success of evangelism. Since ours is an evangelical church you will fit into it very well. As regards your theology degree, you are now the Vice Master of Serampore College Council to which about 49 theological colleges are affiliated. You need not hold a degree in theology to became a pastor." I listened to his encouraging words but was perplexed about my becoming a pastor.

In the meantime, two of his sons Samuel Chetti (Sam) and Daniel Chetti (Danny) were visiting their parents in Calcutta. The pastor wanted me to meet them and hear from them about the points I had raised with him. I met both of them at a mutually convenient date and time. Both of them quoted many instances of USA where Baptist pastors went for theological studies after becoming pastors. I told them "What is possible in USA is not possible in India and I would not like to go for studies after becoming a pastor."

Nevertheless, it was becoming difficult for me to set aside the request. So both Putul and I started praying very fervently to know God's will and to know whether God is calling me to be a pastor.

In December 1990, after long waiting in prayer, I was challenged by the Spirit to accept the request of the pastor to be his successor. We then telephoned our two daughters in Delhi and told them all that had happened and wanted to know their views on my becoming the pastor of Circular Road. Both of them were taken by surprise and gave their consent.

I met the pastor and informed him of my willingness to be his successor. Pastor and his wife Padma were excited to know this decision and both pastor and I prayed together and gave thanks to God for this opportunity.

The pastor immediately started working on completing the ecclesiastical practices of the Baptist Church for my induction as a pastor and for the ordination. He also wanted that I should resign immediately and take over the charge from him. I informed him very politely that my resignation and release from the position I occupy as Managing Director in the Government of India Undertaking was neither easy nor simple. According to terms of appointment, I have to give a three months notice after which Ministry of Steel will obtain clearance from Chief Vigilance Commissioner, Director, CBI, Department of Personnel, Government of India and finally the consent of the Prime Minister's office. These steps are the followed during the appointments and termination of services of all functional directors, managing directors and chairmen's of Government of India Undertakings. Therefore, we have to prayerfully await for my release from service. I also informed that a minimum of 3 months from the day I submit my letter of resignation to the secretary (steel) is necessary for my release. I also appraised him that the present secretary (steel) has been transferred and the new incumbent to this post is the Chief Secretary, Bihar who was likely to join on 26th December 1990. I could, therefore, submit my resignation to him on 2nd Jan. 1991 at the earliest.

I prepared my resignation letter very prayerfully dating it 1st January 1991 and planned a visit to Delhi on 2nd Jan 1991 by a morning flight. It was hard to get an appointment because he had just joined and had many things to attend to. I got appointment to meet him at 5.30 p.m. on the same day. The secretary (steel) thought that I was making a courtesy call. He said that he was quite happy to see me visit him like this and later on would like to talk about what I do and so on and so forth. To this, I told him the reason for my visit was that I had to submit my resignation letter personally to him. He took and read it and returned it and asked, "Are you having any problem with your wife? How many children do you have and what are they doing?" I replied to his queries but he said, " You take this letter back and everything in your family will get settled soon. I would like to meet you next week." I returned disappointed, for my purpose was not fulfilled.

I told to myself, "God, it is your will that I resign. Why then this hindrance?" Anyway, I asked the P.S. of the secretary (steel) to fix a time for me next week.

The new secretary (Steel) Mr. B.C. Das was a perfect gentleman, soft spoken and very polite in his manners. This was very comforting to me.

Since there was no information about my next appointment till 10th January 1991, I called the P.S. and reminded him to fix my appointment. He later informed me that, the meeting was fixed for 23rd January at 2.30 p.m.

As I entered the chamber, the Secretary welcomed me. He offered tea and enquired about my wife, daughters and problems in the family. Then, he asked my relationship with the Union (CITU). He then said, " I have gone through your performance records and also got opinion about you from my predecessors. Since everything is favorable, I am thinking of promoting you to become chairman in one of the public sector undertakings by the end of March 1991. I have discussed this with the Steel Minister Mr. Ashok Sen and he has agreed. So please do not press your resignation." At this point, I decided to reveal the purpose of my resignation. I said, "Sir, I am a Christian and would like to serve the church when I am released." He again said, "Think seriously." I came back finding it hard to get across to the secretary. I requested his P.S. to fix an appointment for me again as early as possible.

On 28th January 1991 at 6 p.m., I met Mr. B. C. Das yet again. He asked "Pramanik have you changed your mind?" I promptly replied "No." He took the letter from my hand and endorsed it to joint secretary to process. But he said something more. (I shall be retiring after 3 years and shall go back to my home state to work for the development in rural areas. I do not like to stay here in Delhi and do consultation work as most of us do after retirement.) I came to know later from my office in Calcutta that when Mr. B. C. Das visited, he did enquire to know whether I had actually joined the church.

I came straight to the concerned joint secretary and informed him all that had happened and wanted him to settle all formalities of clearance by 31st March because my resignation letter was dated 1.1.1991. He did not like to listen to this request. Then I persuaded him in Oriya because he was an IAS officer from U.P. but Orissa cadre and knew Oriya language. He assured me that he would try his best but could not give an assurance for my release on 31.3.1991.

On the other side, my pastor was busy finalizing my induction and ordination starting from the first week of April. I did not know how to reconcile the time of laying down my office and taking over pastoral responsibilities.

I thanked God, when the joint secretary called me on 30th March and requested me to wait till 9th April when he was sure of issuing the release letter and I could hand over charge on 10th April 1991. I informed the pastor of my release date. He then reset the dates for my induction and ordination.

I thought of breaking the news of my resignation and release first in Bombay because it is the place of all the important steel industrialists. I planned a visit to Bombay on 9th April morning and requested the regional manager of Bombay office to arrange a dinner in "The Oberoi Bombay" on 9th April evening and to invite all CEO's of the companies with whom we have business dealings.

After the dinner, I announced that I would be relinquishing my post next day, the 10th April 1991. There was commotion and I could hear someone saying, "Mr. Pramanik has gone mad to resign at a time when his organization is at the height of achievement and profit." They requested me to come for a farewell to Bombay for which they would send me the air-ticket and make other arrangements for my stay. I was invited for the farewell on 23rd April, when I was already a pastor.

On the morning of 10th April, I was back in Calcutta to sign papers for handing over and completing other formalities. All the formalities were arranged the same evening as I was not that keen on coming back the next morning.

I went to the manse on 11th April and met the pastor and observed his method of working and enquired more about my responsibilities as a pastor. The pastor had fixed my induction on 21st April, 1991 and the ordination service on 28th April. I came to know that the ordination service would be an important function consisting 10 Baptist pastors belonging to various churches of the Ordination Council. They belonged to different states - one each from Assam, Andhra Pradesh, Bihar, Kerala, Nagaland, New Delhi, West Bengal and three from Orissa. It was important for the pastors of Orissa to be present where Putul and I grew up. They would report to the council about our family and church background in the early years of our lives. The Ordination Committee consisted of four pastors of the council with Rev. Dr. Imo Iyer as the Secretary.

I was asked by the pastor to prepare my testimony of "conversion" and "my call" to become the pastor. I submitted "my testimony" and a note on "my call" to be a pastor much before the induction service of 21st April. After I was inducted as the pastor in the morning service of 21st April, I had a very peculiar experience. After the service, late John Peacock, my close friend and church secretary and late Lilian Roy, an elderly and graceful lady, who was the treasurer of the church, addressed me as pastor. Likewise, my pastor and his wife Padma also addressed me as pastor instead of "Mohit", I then realized the position to which God has elevated me and how important are the pastoral responsibilities. The Council met on 26th April evening and again on 27th April evening. They studied "my testimony" and "my call" to examine my suitability as a pastor. I also meet the Ordination Committee on 27th April morning in a session.

The ordination service on 28th April was a solemn occasion. Some of my relatives including Putul's parents had come from Cuttack to attend this service. Many church leaders including the Bishop of Calcutta, Rt. Rev. D. C. Gorai also attended.

My pastor, late Rev. Dr. C. Devasahayam was the presiding pastor. The service opened with prayer by the pastor of Sambalpur Baptist Church followed by Dr. Imo Iyer reading the report to the congregation. After receiving positive response that I was acceptable to be their pastor, the service continued.

Rev. Subodh Sahu brought the ordination message followed by Rev. Dr. Robert Reid, pastor, DBF, New Delhi brought the message on "charge to the church". Rev. Lloyd Raine, pastor, Carey Baptist Church, Calcutta brought a message on "challenge to the candidate". After the ordination service, there was a time of rejoicing and thanksgiving to God over tea at the lawn of the manse. This enabled me to acquaint myself with many church leaders and pastors in Calcutta who I did not know.

On 29th April morning, I went to meet the pastor in manse. The pastor was sick and bed-ridden. I met him in his bed room and prayed for his recovery. I returned home sad for the sickness of the pastor. After a few days, he was detected of cancer. So, his departure to Madras in the 1st week of May was postponed and treatment started in Calcutta. God listened to the prayers of many and his condition improved so much so that he could move around. He was released from the hospital to continue treatment in Vellore.

A farewell meeting was arranged for him and his wife Padma on 1st June 1991. The pastor shared his joyful experiences while serving the church. He then blessed the congregation, Putul and me to serve the church in love and in the unity of the Spirit. He requested for prayer for his early recovery.

In the farewell service, I exhorted the congregation expounding the Scripture portion from Hebrews 13:7-17. The text of the message was verses 7 and 17, which read "Remember your leaders those who spoke the Word of God, consider the outcome of their way of life and imitate their faith" and "Obey your leaders and submit to their authority."

The pastor and his wife Padma had planned their departure to Madras on 6th June. Their son Danny and his wife Sarah had come to accompany them to Madras. Danny was a professor at Gurukul Theological Research and Educational Institute in Madras at that time. They all left but did leave behind a great history and his exemplary life as the pastor for all of us to cherish and practice.

We shifted to the manse on 7th June 1991 morning and started our work of responsibility as the pastor of this historical church.

1.2 Why I took retirement?

My journey as pastor at Circular Road started with much joy, expecting God to grant His enabling grace to overcome my deficiencies and inadequacies in the pastoral ministry. But no wonder, very soon I faced hardships and disappointments in some areas of my ministry. I comforted myself thinking "I did turn-aside my earlier business of life and responded to God's divine claim to be a pastor; why should I be burdened with such small things?" The Spirit of God encouraged me as

I heard God's voice challenging and encouraging me again and again "Somewhere in life there is a voice for which every thing else has to be given up." I was also reminded of this challenging promise of William Carey-

> "Expect great things from God
> Attempt great things for God"

We continued our ministry without fear and doubt-focusing our attention on Jesus for strength and help. God helped us to get concerned and involved in the joys and sorrows, sicknesses and troubles of the congregation. We met them, prayed with them, edified them and rejoiced with them in their family celebrations.

Putul was engaged in nurturing and directing the youth fellowship and the Sunday school teachers. Thus, a very open and fruitful relationship was established with the worshippers. The congregation grew with God's blessing and grace.

In the second year of my ministry, God spoke to both of us in our private prayer time very clearly in a vision to labour steadfastly to accomplish the task of planting a sister church in the city of Calcutta. We had realised that this was a hard task. But we started praying believing that God would help the church to accomplish this project. At the outset, we requested the deacons and then the congregation to pray for guidance and direction.

In early 1994, the deacons and the congregation considered appointing their Bengali speaking missionaries withdrawing three from other states. The new missionaries started working in South of Calcutta because they were acquainted with some families who lived there. Two of them were girls and one was a boy who had completed B. Th. in Mark Buntain Theological College, Calcutta. The two girls were trained in evangelism by "Youth with a Mission". These three missionaries were properly equipped to win souls. My wife and I used to meet them in the manse every Tuesday afternoon. They used to share their sorrows, problems and challenges but were prepared to face difficulties. We used to pray together and instruct and encourage them in their ministry.

No sooner, by God's grace and blessings, we had about 30-40 people including children who were willing to gather to worship on Sundays. We agreed to open the Jullian hall (social hall) of the church for the service every Sunday afternoon. This group travelled long distances to reach Circular Road but this did not deter them. They longed to worship. They enjoyed singing choruses and hymns in Bengali, Hindi and English. This group consisted of "Christians" who had never attended church service earlier and the others were from Hindu background including Brahmins. They were "seekers" who belonged to lower middle class families. The "seekers", after some teaching accepted the truth of the Scripture and were ready to accept Jesus as their Savior. But the hurdles they faced were to throw away idols from their homes and for the married women to discontinue using vermilion and "tilak" from their foreheads. These women had another difficulty with their husbands to remove "red" and "white" bangles which they considered similar to wedding rings of Christians.

Our God is faithful and the Spirit helped eight men and women including a Brahmin couple to publicly declare their faith in Christ by taking water baptism. The first baptism of the eight was a great day of rejoicing both by the English speaking congregation and the newly emerged Bengali speaking congregation. The baptism was held in the baptistry of the Circular Road with much joy and praise to God.

Slowly, the group was growing in number. It was, therefore, decided to shift the place of worship to a convenient location in South Calcutta. We hired a hall every Sunday for evening worship from the "Youth with a Mission". The need for at least one more missionary was realised and another missionary girl was appointed. It was marvellous to see how God was blessing the labour of love and work of faith. When baptised members were added to this congregation, the need for a pastor to lead the communion service arose. I had to go to South Calcutta once a month to conduct communion service and also attend both the services at the Circular Road, the same Sunday. God gave me enough strength and zeal to do it joyfully. The fellowship with this congregation and was a very rewarding experience. Since the young missionary boy who had already worked for about six years, had B.Th. degree and was married to one of the missionary girls (a convert) of the team, it became easy to consider him to be the assistant pastor for the Bengali congregation. He was inducted as the shepherd of this sister church in January 2002; much before my departure in June 2002. By then the baptised members had increased to 22 and many more were unable to get the baptism because of social stigma and religious practices of married women.

The English congregation had already started raising funds through "faith promise giving" to build them a church for worship. More than adequate money was already raised within 2 years by 2000 to buy a plot of land and to build a structure for worship, without asking for any support money from outside.

Putul and I knew that God had already blessed our ministry and the congregation had grown spiritually and economically. A sister church has been established. My wife and I were growing physically weak to work all the seven days a week. It was time for us to make way for a young pastor to take over. We informed the deacons of our intention to take retirement. We started looking for a successor. The search did not succeed and we decided to advertise the need for a pastor in "Light of Life" and "AIMS" magazines. There was good response but only one was found suitable for an interview. After completing the selection process and on receiving good report about the candidate and his family, the congregation agreed to issue an appointment letter. The pastor designate and his family agreed to arrive in Calcutta in April 2002 as soon as the schools of their children closed. Since I had agreed to stay for another two months for the new pastor to work with me, we decided to leave Calcutta in June 2002.

We gave thanks and glory to God for being with us in the ministry for 11 years and granting us the grace to accomplish all the tasks. Above all, planting a sister church for the new converts in South Calcutta was accomplished. We had realised that our time for departure had come and that with new and young leadership the church will reach greater heights.

The deacons and the congregation arranged a farewell meeting for us in the 1st week of June 2002 as well as to introduce my successor to the gathering presented there. This proved to be an excellent evening as the deacons conducted the meeting with much dignity and love.

I responded, as my turn came in the farewell meeting. I said, "My heart is full, so my mouth refuses to speak. I reaffirmed that we love each and every one of you and shall continue our love even when we are gone. We will uphold the congregation in prayer for both spiritual and physical growth." Then, I gave a short message from 2 Peter 1:12-21 and the text was verse 15. It reads "And I will make every effort to see that after my departure you will always be able to remember these things" that I have shared and preached to them. This is the reward we have received for our labour of love and work of faith.

Before I close, I would like to mention something, I overheard in my farewell meeting. This has a spiritual meaning and trust you will value it.

One church leader over the fellowship tea remarked, "Pastor Pramanik is mad to leave when under his leadership there is all round growth in the church and a sister church has been planted." As I heard this, I was reminded of a similar remark an industrialist made at my farewell meeting in Bombay 11 years ago. I realised 'Yes, we are in a mad world but God knows who are mad and who are wise and prudent.' Unless human heart is transformed, it is the same whether your are a church leader or a businessman who belong to the world.

My pastoral ministry was the most glorious period in my life span which surpasses all the position and power I enjoyed in my secular service.

May this testimony inspire and embolden someone to be a pastor without considering this as a job but as God's call to serve Him and His people faithfully in the church.

Chapter - 2

A Note From the Author

Incorporating my testimony in this book, which contains the summary of select sermons, is an afterthought. Many of my friends requested me to write my testimony addressing two vital issues – How I became a pastor resigning from a high position in a secular job and also why I took retirement from church when my congregation and deacons were reluctant to let me go. Both are significant aspects of my life and it would be useful and interesting for the readers to know. I, therefore, decided to write this testimony after much prayer trusting that it will encourage others to serve the cause of our Lord in His Kingdom. It is my prayer that my testimony may inspire someone to heed the call of God for pastoral ministry in a mainline evangelical church. This is a need that is not being met adequately at present.

    The summary of selected sermons are of 25 to 35 minutes duration of biblical illustrations and historical background. They have been classified according to the spiritual growth of a Christian from the time of conversion. This journey starts with living faith in Christ. As the root of your faith goes deep down, the best of your faith is seen up in your life. But please remember when your faith is tested by God, you are being grounded deeper in your faith and in your relationship with God; being perfected to dispel fear, doubt and mistrust in the Lord. Therefore, watch out who is testing your faith. Is it lifting you up to God or is it pulling you down to earthly comforts and pleasures? If you are being tested by Satan, he is trying to bring out the worst in you. But our God is faithful to honour His promises. So continue to remain in Him. "Fix our eyes upon Jesus, the Author and Perfecter of our faith" (Hebrews 12:2a).

The spiritual nourishment for growth evolves around your devotional life – in worship and in meditating on the Word of God. As you grow, you devote yourself more and more to fellowship with godly people and serve the Lord in your church life. As a disciple of Christ, you ought to shine before men in your thoughts and actions and people will see your "good" deeds to praise God and not you. Trust in the promises of Jesus and claim them for your spiritual and emotional comfort.

"Remain in me, and I will remain in you. No branch can bear fruit by itself, it must remain in the vine" (John 15: 4a).

"In this world you will have trouble. But take heart! I have overcome the world" (John 16: 33b).

For those friends who are confident of their rock – like faith, a word of caution (1 Cor. 10:12). Your faith may turn to sand when unpleasant and unwanted feelings and emotions will catch you unawares to devastate your spiritual life. Again, I will remind you of the unshakable promises of God to stand firm against such hard times in your sojourn in Christian life. Claim the following promises for your spiritual power and strength.

"Who shall separate us from the love of Christ? Shall trouble or hardship or persecution or famine or nakedness or danger or sword?" "No, in all these things we are more than conquerors through Him who loved us" (Romans 8:35 & 37).

"In everything, by prayer and petition, with thanksgiving, present your requests to God. And the peace of God, which transcends all understanding, will guard your hearts and your minds in Christ Jesus" (Philippians 4: 6b and 7).

"I can do everything through Him (Jesus Christ) who gives me strength" (Philippians 4: 13).

Always remember, *"a quitter never wins and a winner never quits."* You are an ultimate victor and not a victim of circumstances.

Finally, to experience the joy and peace of salvation in all its fullness follow the steps, I suggest below to be perfect in the sight of God in this imperfect world·

- **Develop strong appetite for prayer.** Ask God first for His Kingdom and His righteousness to come on earth and all other things shall be given to you as well. The more you love and honour God, the less you ask for yourself in prayer.
- **Develop the practice of reading and meditating on the Word of God daily.** Cultivate this as a regular practice to fight the snares of the devil during the day.
- **Develop intimate personal relationship with God, the Holy Spirit.** He imparts strength and power, joy and peace, love and compassion and the living hope to enjoy the blessedness of eternal life.

Before you start reading the summary of sermons may I request you to read carefully the following to have true realization of truth contained there in.

> *"The sermon itself is the main thing… the sacred anointing upon the preacher and the divine power applying the truth to the hearer … these are definitely more important than any details of manner."*
>
> *- Charles H. Spurgeon*

Another story told by an elderly and saintly lady Beta Shyrick. She was a Methodist missionary in China. She eventually left the mission and became a co-worker with Watchman Nee. She went with young Watchman Nee to hear a great preacher. After listening to the great preacher very carefully, Beta Shyrick told something very profound to Nee. She was Nee's mentor at that time.

"Many years ago this preacher had a profound experience with Jesus Christ. It is experience that changed his life and brought brokenness into his life but he has been living on that experience and preaching on that experience ever since. He does not have an up-to-date present walk with the Lord. He is operating on a past encounter with God."

Watchman Nee then began to realize the necessity and the *importance of having a living experimental relationship with Jesus when all doctrine, all power, all practice, all concepts, all creeds pale into insignificance and comes to one point: centrality of Jesus in all things.*

Apostle Paul tells us in 2 Timothy 4: 3, "For the time will come when men will not put up with sound doctrine. Instead to suit their own desires, they will gather around them a great number of teachers to say what their itching ears want to hear."

Worship God to hear His voice and not the preacher's oratory in the worship.

In closing, I would recommend you to read two messages that I brought to my congregation in July 1991 in the third month of taking charge as pastor entitled, *"The Church that dares to change"* and my last message before my departure in June 2002 entitled, *"Arise, Shine"* (both found in Chapter 4, section 4.4.3 on Revival). Trust you will be blessed as you read them.

Chapter – 3

"Lord, make me your own"
(Redeemed or regenerated life)

3.1 Living faith

Significance of our faith
Hebrews 11: 1-27

1. **Our faith has great God:** Our God is in the beginning (Gen.1:1). He is Alpha and Omega (Rev.1:8). He is the Creator of the universe (Heb.11:3) and re-creator of saved sinners (Eph. 2:10). Only a fool says that there is no God (Psalm 14:1). Faith ought to be great since our God is great (Gal. 2:20 and Isaiah 40:28-31).

2. **Our faith has great commitment:** Response to the great God needs great commitment. It costs much to make commitments. Paul had to suffer much to honor Christ in his life and ministry (Acts 9: 16 and 2 Cor.11: 23-27). Noah, Moses and Abraham honored God at great cost because of their faith in God (Heb.11: 7, 8 and 24-27).

3. **Our faith has great trials:** Abraham's faith was tested in a great trial (Heb.11: 17-19). He received God's blessings for his faith in God to be called "friend of God". Our God does not allow trials and temptations to overpower those who trust in Him (1 Cor.10:13).

4. **Our faith has great inspiration:** Christ is our inspiration for He perfects our faith in Him (Heb.12: 2). The promises of God inspire us to remain faithful to Him (Heb.13: 5).

5. **Our faith has great reward:** Whatever may be the cost, our faith has great reward (1 Peter 1:7). Believers in Christ see the reward of crown even now from a distance (Rev. 3:11 & Heb. 11:13). Faith and faithful service are not in vain (1 Cor.15:58). This is our living hope of eternal life (1 Peter 4:13).

Pilgrimage of faith
Micah 7: 8-13

Christian life is a journey of pilgrimage...full of trials and temptations. However, faith and hope in risen Christ empowers us to overcome them and sustain faith. Micah experienced ultimate victory because of his faithfulness to God. We can hope for ultimate victory, if only we trust God all through the journey.

1. **Pilgrimage of faith is a troublesome one (vs. 8):** Micah recognized the presence of the enemy but he continued to rejoice in the Lord without fear. He overcame the problems. Micah's hope of ultimate victory was because of his faith. Jesus said, "In this world you will have problems. But take heart, I have overcome the world" (John 6:33).

2. **Pilgrimage of faith is an imperfect one (vs. 9):** Confession of sins lead to victorious living. Holding on to faith restores fellowship with God. Abraham and David were restored to God in spite of their imperfections in life. We may stumble in the path of faith... but we are perfected in our weakness by the Spirit (2 Cor.12: 9)

3. **Pilgrimage of faith is in trusting God (vs. 8 and 9):** We may fall, yet we can rise, if we trust God. We shall experience God's grace and mercy when we claim His promises on God's conditions of forgiveness of our sins and remain obedient to His commandments.

4. **Pilgrimage of faith leads to eternal life (vs. 10-12):** Jesus will restore all broken relationship and fellowship when we submit (surrender) to God in full trust in Him (Joel 2:25).

Pilgrimage of faith
Psalm 51:1-19

Christian's destiny is heaven. They are only pilgrims here on earth. The journey on earth is full of temptations, unwanted experiences and hard decisions. King David for his unfailing faith in God sought God's love, grace and mercy to live a victorious life even though he had fallen in committing adultery (2 Sam. 12:13).

1. **Pilgrimage of faith is an imperfect one (vs. 1-4):** David stumbled and committed adultery. But he confessed his sin in full repentance and sought God's forgiveness (vs.7-9). God restored him to the joy of salvation (vs.12). Abraham and Peter had stumbled in their faith and God restored them in His love and they rose to move forward in their faith.

2. **Pilgrimage of faith is a troublesome one (vs. 5 and 6):** David acknowledged that circumstances and temptations lead him to take such a terrible sinful decision. Job suffered and lost his children, possessions and his health and yet he did not reject God but worshipped Him (Job 1:20-21). He was blessed to prosper in all aspects of life (Job 42:12-15).

3. **Pilgrimage of faith is in trusting God (vs. 15-17):** Trusting God, David strives to draw closer to Him with a broken and contrite heart. When you strive under Jesus with a broken and contrite heart, you will overcome evil.

4. **Pilgrimage of faith assures living hope (vs. 18):** Claiming the promises of God, David is sure to enjoy the blessings

of an eternal life and stay with the Lord forever (Psalm 23: 6).

Faith is the key to living hope and living hope is the key to living faith.

The secret of perfecting our faith
Hebrews 11: 32-40

Our faith is not philosophy but theology. The object of our faith is Jesus Christ. Perfecting faith in Christ does not refer to sinless perfection but commands us to press forward to reach the goal set before us. Apostle Paul says, "I press on towards the goal to win the prize for which God has called me heavenwards in Christ Jesus" (Phil.3:14).

Our faith strives to reach the goal (perfection) in two stages.

1. **Primary faith:** Our faith in Christ's death on the cross and shedding of His blood redeems us from the guilt and penalty of sin (Rom. 5:9). This faith is primary and essence for the forgiveness of sin (Heb. 10:22 & Matt. 9:6 & 22).

2. **Perfecting faith:** There are four ways by which God perfects our faith in granting us power to overcome sin. The power of God was demonstrated in the resurrection of Jesus Christ. With the indwelling Spirit, sin will have no dominion over saved sinners (Rom. 8:1).

    a) *Adoration faith.* It is a proof of our faith. It is two fold:
       * To bring our bodies as a living sacrifice to God (Rom.12: 2).
       * To praise and thank God in songs, hymns, prayer and worship (Eph.5: 19 and 20)

    b) *Adventure faith.* (Heb. 11: 7-10; 17-19; 23-28). Noah, Abraham and Moses went out on adventures to carry out God's command. Their faith was exploited to be confirmed.

c) **Deliverance faith.** (Heb.11: 32-40). God delivered His faithful people- David, Daniel, Hezekiah, Peter, Paul and Silas from persecutions leading even to death.

d) **Disaster faith.** This does not give an answer to our sufferings and pain on earth (Heb. 11:13). Our God is sovereign. He does what pleases Him for His purpose.

Primary faith grants positional perfection to saved sinners. Perfecting faith (all the four) lead to relative perfection of saintly holiness in life and the ultimate perfection will be attained only when we meet the Lord face to face in heaven.

Faith of David; Man after God's own heart
Psalm 16

All the Psalms have captured the deep experience and dream of mankind. They are the mirror which reflects human attitude and emotions. Psalms act as a spiritual mirror or a spiritual thermometer. Therefore read one Psalm a day and practice the teachings in your life to be spiritually healthy. Psalm 16 reflects David's character and the blessings he received in his life.

1. **His faith was personal:** This Psalm is full of personal relationship with God as 'me' and 'my' God, 'keep me safe', 'Lord counsels me', 'God is my Creator and my Saviour'. These personal experiences confirm his deep faith in God.

2. **His faith was absolute:** He puts his trust in God, meaning he had no one else to turn to. His faith was absolute. He says, "I shall not be moved (shaken)" and "I have a delightful inheritance". God works in everything and in all circumstances (Rom. 8:28) if you love Him.

3. **His faith was habitual:** Faith cannot be developed overnight or experienced for a particular matter or circumstance. David says, " I have set the Lord *always* before me." Faith must be cultivated, developed and exercised always for growing into spiritual maturity.

Warriors of faith
Hebrews 11:1-7

The Bible records some warriors of faith in Hebrew chapter 11. They exhibit their great faith through their worship, walking with the Lord and working according to God's will.

1. **Abel worshiped by faith (vs. 4):** By faith, Abel accepted the revealed way of worship and accordingly he offered the first portion of his flock. God had revealed the way of salvation that is only through the shedding of the blood (Gen. 3:21). Abel brought blood offering by faith and he confessed that he was a sinner. This is the acceptable way of worship. It is the blood of Christ that grants us the redeeming grace of God to worship Him in spirit and in truth.

2. **Enoch walked by faith (vs. 5-6):** He walked with God so closely and so intimately that his relationship with God enabled Enoch to be with the Lord without tasting physical death (Gen. 5:21-24). His faith in God is demonstrated when he prophesied about the second coming of Christ (Jude 14 and15).

3. **Noah worked by faith (vs. 7):** He followed God in every step of his life in the midst of several odds (Gen.6 : 9b). His absolute faith in God sustained him to work according to all that God commanded him to do (Gen. 6:22).

A true worshipper of God (John 4:23-24), walks closely with God, works honestly and sincerely by faith for the glory of God.

When does faith collapse?
Judges 16: 1-30; 1 Cor. 10: 12 & 13

Samson is a tragic example of collapse of faith (1 Cor. 10:12). There are three ways by which sin (Satan) makes you fall. But God is faithful and He will not let you fall (1 Cor. 10:13).

1. **You should always be aware that the devil's main aim is to pull down your faith in Christ (Judges 16:4,5):** Look at Joseph's temptations (Gen.39: 7 and 8) and how Joseph overcame them (Gen. 39: 9 and 10). There is no higher spiritual life from which your faith will stand without collapsing. King David committed adultery (2 Sam. 11: 2-5) though God had chosen him to be the King of Israel.

2. **Backsliding or loss of faith does not happen suddenly (Judges 16 :15& 16):** It happens gradually. So be alert always to examine your words, thoughts and deeds. Examine who are your friends and with whom you have relationship; examine what books you read and how you spend time to relax.

3. **The collapse of faith is invisible if there is dichotomy of faith(Judges 16:20):** There is little conviction of your faith even when you may freely proclaim faith. In such a position what you say and what you do is hypocrisy. There is deliberate disobedience to God's commandments. But there is no situation or position from which the Lord cannot save and pull you up. Samson did not trust God but trusted his friends and advisors but David returned to God.

When does faith become trust?
Mark 10: 46-52; James 2:14-17

Faith must be tested to be trusted. Faith becomes trust when it is genuine. Thoughts and deeds are outward proof of the reality or genuineness of faith (James 2: 14-17). *Your way of life is the testimony of your faith.*

1. **Highest regard for Jesus (vs. 47):** Jesus is the Lord of your life and you obey His Lordship in your life. You declare Him as your personal Saviour and you act to prove that Jesus is the God incarnate – the Son of God.

2. **Humility in honoring Jesus (vs. 47):** When you are helpless and look to Jesus for help, trusting in God's power and strength, you will overcome howsoever the situation appears hard and impossible. In honoring Jesus, you are blessed. Nothing is impossible with God (Luke 1:37 and Matt. 19:26).

3. **Faith overcomes obstructions (vs. 48):** There are many situations which may lead you to give up your faith in Christ and you will be tempted to look to others for help. But trust in Jesus and pray fervently and you will triumph over all the situations and circumstances that are troublesome. Blind Bartimaeus received his sight despite all obstructions.

4. **Faith leads to specific request to Jesus (vs. 51):** You should be sure of what to ask and whom to ask and wait patiently till you receive. Bartimaeus shouted, "Jesus have mercy on me." How deep is your prayer to Jesus?

5. **Faith helps to follow Jesus all the way (vs. 52):** When your faith becomes trust, you follow Jesus all the way of your life as Bartimaeus did.

Prove your faith in love and compassion
Eph. 2:8-18

The people around you want to see your faith in and through your life as to how you live with your family, your church and your community. Your work in all spheres of life proves the reality of your faith.

1. **Our faith is neither costly nor traditional:** Faith based on superstitions and prejudice is the faith of people who seek favors from an unknown god. It is ritualistic faith. It costs them travel, treasure (money) and time.

2. **Our faith is not based on good works:** Right relationship of a saved sinner with God (Jesus) compels to do good work (Eph. 2:10). **Work is not the root of salvation but work is the fruit of salvation.**

3. **Our faith is dynamic and effective:** Faith in Christ makes a difference in your style of living. Therefore, it is not by segregation that you establish your faith, but through your words, thoughts and deeds in love and compassion for others (2 Cor. 5:14,15). This is how you demonstrate your faith to others. It is impossible to prove your faith without "good works" which is pleasing and acceptable to God.

Therefore, when your faith leads you to act in love and compassion you can proclaim the gospel without hindrance (Matt. 9:36-38). In a pluralistic society where Christ is marginalized as one among several other gods, we should be tolerant towards such people instead of compromising with them or getting agitated. We also need not decry what is good ethically of other religions. Only then, you will have insight and the power of discernment to bear fruit and win souls for the Kingdom of God even in hostile situations (2 Timothy 2:7 & 9).

Privileges of our faith
Romans 8: 31-39

Those who trust in Jesus, they are more than conquerors through Him, against all confusion and chaos, earthquakes and cyclones, hunger and poverty, wars and threats of war. In the midst of all these, not only do they overcome but they also grow in their spiritual life and commitment to God - What is more, they look forward to eternal life.

Apostle Paul exclaimed, "what a wretched man I am" to live in this world; but immediately, he declares in thanksgiving to God that through Jesus, he has been rescued from misery (Rom. 7:24,25).

What are our privileges ?

1. **Unquestionable presence (vs. 31):** Focus onto Jesus and not to your friends when things are troublesome and fearful. God's Spirit in you will drive away your unbelief, and grant you the confidence of His presence (Exo. 33:14 & Psalm 37: 3-7).

2. **Unlimited provisions (vs. 32):** God made the best provision for the entire mankind in His plan of salvation which assures eternal life to all those who trust in the saving grace of Jesus Christ. God meets all your needs according to His glorious riches in Christ Jesus. (Phil. 4:19). Claim this promise on God's condition of forgiveness of sins.

3. **Unfathomable pardon (vs. 33):** Trust that the blood of Jesus Christ that washes all the stains of sin in your life and sets you free from condemnation and eternal fire. You are free indeed from the guilt and power of sin and you rejoice in the Lord for such a priceless pardon. Jesus came to do what you could have never done for yourself; the work of reconciliation bringing you into relationship with a pardoning and Holy God.

4. **Unceasing prayer (Vs. 34):** Jesus is interceding with God for all the believers that they shall not be condemned by anyone.
5. **Unfailing love (Vs. 35,38):** Nothing, absolutely nothing can separate the believers from the love of God who has poured out His love lavishly on His children (1 John 3:1).

Faith – Rest
Matt. 11: 28-30

"Rest" has threefold meaning: blessing, peace and joy. Jesus invites us to receive this "Rest" which is an antidote to fear and doubt, stress and strain, frustration and weary.

1. **Rest of "Salvation":** Those who accept Jesus personally as Saviour and Lord of their lives, they are cleansed by the blood of Jesus and have received forgiveness of sin. They are blessed with the joy of salvation (Psalm 51:12) and the peace of God guards their heart and minds in Jesus Christ (Phil. 4: 7). This is peace and joy of salvation.

2. **Rest of "Spiritual growth":** Jesus said, "Take my yoke upon you and learn of me." Unless you are yoked with Jesus and walk with Him, you cannot have fellowship with Him and it will be impossible to grow in spiritual life. In studying the Word of God and hearing His voice in prayer and worship, you have fellowship with Him. Fellowship and communion with Jesus grants spiritual power and growth in spiritual life.

3. **Rest of "Peace" (Daniel 6:17-23):** Daniel could rest peacefully in the den of lions because of his faith of God's presence with him. Whereas Darius, the king was restless even though he was in a luxurious palace. Peace, joy and blessings are supernatural gifts of God and are the essence of "faith - rest" in Christ.

   Jesus promised this rest; claim it.

How deep is the root of your faith?
Heb. 11: 1-40

Christian life revolves in and around faith. Faith looks at the immutability of God's Word and not at the uncertainty of ever-changing world. Faith is a fact not a feeling. Trust in God is the very heart of faith.

1. **Faith is personal:** For salvation, faith is a personal trust (Rom. 4: 5, Gal. 3:6).

2. **Faith gives confidence:** When we pray we have confidence in God that He will grant our request (1 John 4:13-16). Faith drops its letter in the post box and lets it go (Heb. 11:1).

3. **Faith is the working principle of Christian life:**

    a) *Active faith.* It gives thanks for a promise, which is not yet received. Our spiritual power is proportionate to our faith (John 11:41 and James 5:16b).

    b) *Imperfect faith.* Here faith calls for some feelings and the Word of God is set aside or ignored (Judges 6:17). Do not be influenced by the words of the people of this world but by the Word and promises of God.

    c) *Little faith.* It is when faith looks at problems instead of God (Matt.14: 29, 30).

    d) *Desperate faith.* When a Christian is at his/her wits end, he or she does not despair but leaves it in the hands of God. Jesus looked to the Father in the garden of Gethsemane (Lk. 22:42).

    e) *Prevailing faith.* Faith prays earnestly even in hopeless circumstances as did Elijah (James 5:17,18). The faith of three Hebrew boys on God saved their lives when they were thrown in the fiery furnace (Daniel 3 : 24-27).

f) **Glorious faith.** (Heb. 11:8-10). Abraham enjoyed the promised land as his inheritance because he had unfailing faith in God and was known as a "friend of God".

3.2 Sufferings and trials of faith
Crises of faith
Job 1: 13-22; 42: 1-6 and 10-17

Our faith in God is tested in trying circumstances. Faith is perfected in trials and sufferings. The story of Job tells us of disasters that overtook him. Job did not find answers to his suffering and pain, but he found God and worshipped Him (Job 1:20). In the life of Job, we find three answers to sustain faith and to come out victorious:

1. **A theological answer:** In the midst of tragedy, Job found God to worship Him (Job 1:20). He acknowledged that God is sovereign and said, "My eyes have seen Him" (Job 42:5). You can see and meet God while going through such trials and sufferings: *So, do not waste your sorrows and pains. God has a redemptive purpose and gives meaning to everything He owes.*

2. **A psychological answer:** When the mind is uplifted to God in counting His blessings in your own life and family life, you realize that God is "good." Job did not decide to go away from God when his wife and friends so advised him, he counted the blessings of God in his life. Our faith ought to transform our mind, only then can we count the blessings of God (Rom.12: 1,2).

3. **An emotional answer:** Emotion ought to be purified by the Spirit. This is an ongoing process. Those who overcome trying circumstances in life, they alone can defend their faith and will not be a victim of emotions and feelings but a victor (Job 1:21).

When storms come in life
Mark 4:35-41

Jesus taught His disciples not to have "little faith" in God (Matthew 8:26). He took them through a storm to test their faith. The disciples failed in this trial of faith.

1. **They had doubt (vs. 35):** Jesus said, "Let us go to the other side." This was a promise for a safe journey to the other side. The disciples doubted this promise of Jesus to go to the "other side" of the sea (vs. 37). Likewise, the serpent (Satan) brought doubt to Eve to commit the first sin. The disciples doubted when the storm came even when they were sailing with Jesus in the same boat.

2. **They had fear (vs. 31):** They lost their faith in the face of a storm. Fear hinders spiritual growth. Jesus told the disciples, "you still have no faith." The Scripture says, "Be still and know that I am God" (Psalm 46: 10). Instead of fear and doubt, we ought to wait on the Lord patiently.

3. **They wondered (vs. 41):** Having seen so many miracles of Jesus, the disciples were yet wondering. If you too have experienced the miracle of God in your life, you need to be His witness to all your friends and relations of the miracles that God is doing in your and your family life. *There is always a divine purpose of each miracle.* Testing of your faith develops perseverance (patience and diligence) so that you may be mature and complete, not lacking anything (James 1:3,4).

You should realize that Jesus is in your boat. He is alive and He is never silent.

> *"We have an anchor, that keeps the soul;*
> *steadfast and sure, while the billons roll;*
> *fastened to the Rock which cannot move;*
> *grounded firm and deep in the Saviour's love"*

The good fight of faith
Eph. 6:10-18

Conviction of faith comes when faith is perfected in fighting spiritual battle or warfare. It is "good" fight because through this you overcome the evil design of Satan. It is an invisible battle but the victory is visible.

The power of the enemy should never be under estimated (vs. 10-12).

1. **Our armours are spiritual:** The armours are truth, righteousness, peace and faith (vs. 14-16).
2. **Our weapon is spiritual:** Equipped with the Word of God and the promises of God, you can overcome the spiritual warfare. Jesus did exactly this in His time of temptation. (Matt. 4: 4, 7&10).
3. **Our action plan of battle is spiritual (1 Sam. 17: 47):** The secret or hidden strength to fight this battle comes from God (Rom. 8: 31-34).
4. **Our victory is spiritual:** Victory is divine peace and joy which transcends all human understanding of rationalism, secularism and pluralism (Phil 4:7 & 3:4-6).
5. **Our reward is spiritual:** Apostle Paul said, " I have fought the good fight, I have finished the race, I have kept the faith, now there is in store for me the crown of righteousness" (2 Timothy 4:7 & 8).

This battle belongs to God but victory comes to those who remain faithful to Jesus.

Sufferings and pain bring glory to God
John 12: 20-33; 1 Peter 4: 12-19

Those who are in Christ will suffer with Christ (Acts 9:5). Those who suffer for Christ without Christ in them, the glory belongs to them and not to Jesus Christ. Jesus died on the cross and the glory of the cross belongs to God (John 12:27). Jesus told of His sufferings and death for giving glory and honour to God's redemptive plan for mankind (John 17:4).

1. **Glorify God in suffering and pain (1 Peter 4:12-13, John 12:23):** Even Peter had not realized the purpose of Jesus' suffering, dying on the cross and His resurrection from the grave (Matt. 16:23). Those who are in Christ, they will suffer for Christ. Jesus revealed to Ananias, " I will show him (Paul) how much he will suffer for my name" (Acts 9:15,16). God was glorified as Paul suffered for the name of Jesus Christ (2 Timothy 2:3, 9 & 10).

   Christians (born again) who belong to Jesus find meaning and purpose in every pain and sufferings that challenges their faith *but the unbelievers waste their pains*. New birth in Christ brings suffering and pain for the glory of God (Heb. 2:10).

2. **Glorify God in following Christ (1 Peter 4:16):** When you glorify God for your personal name and fame, you will surely lose your faith when suffering for Jesus comes. Many disciples left Him when they heard of His suffering and death (John 6:66).

   There is glory in following Jesus, but do not go out of step with Him because the journey with Jesus is hazardous. Jesus promised " Do not let your hearts be troubled and do not be afraid" (John 14: 24). Take refuge in God in times of trouble (Nahum 1:7).

Why should you suffer for Christ?
2 Cor. 1:3-11; 1 Peter 4:12-16; Hebrews 12:7-11

Christians suffer and pass through hardships in life mostly because of their faith in Christ (1 Peter 4: 12,13). Many try to find answers to these difficulties and problems and question- " Why me, Lord?" The right question is – "What is your will and purpose for my suffering, Lord?" You suffer for being a Christian and as you live a Christ like life (John 15: 18-19). For you do not belong to the world and the world hates you.

God has fourfold purpose for the sufferings of Christians:

1. **To be a blessing to others (2 Cor. 1:3):** Once you go through the hardship, you understand it and help a person in a similar situation. As comfort flows from Christ to you so also, through Christ you can comfort others physically, spiritually and emotionally.
2. **To humble you (2 Cor. 1: 8,9):** In certain situations, you may feel helpless even with power, position and wealth with you. God humbles His people in experiencing such situations when they bow down before Him, seeking, His grace and mercy.
3. **To disciple you (Heb. 12: 10):** God disciplines through hardship, so that you will be acceptable in His sight as disciple of Christ. Discipleship produces harvest of righteousness. So, endure hardships as God is in control of your life (Heb. 12:7).
4. **To honor and glorify God (Heb. 12:11):** When God does a miracle in your suffering, His name is glorified. God does not allow hardship, which you cannot bear (1 Cor. 10:13). Through your sufferings, God is glorified as you become a blessing to others.

Your salvation is perfected through sufferings (Heb. 2 : 10b). Sufferings give you hope of eternal life (1 Peter 1:7, 4:13) and insight to discern what is right and what is wrong (2 Tim. 2:7).

Faith is non-negotiable and faith never fails
Daniel 6:1-23

Daniel, a captive in a foreign land stood firm in his faith and worshipped his living God. His faith was non-negotiable even when he was put to uncomfortable, inconvenient and unexpected situations (vs 8, 9). Daniel came out victorious from the lion's den for the glory of his God.

Apostle Paul tells us of his trials and sufferings for his faith in Christ (2 Cor. 11: 23-28). Paul remained faithful till the end to establish churches in Asia- Minor and Europe for God's glory.

1. **Our faith need not be a hindrance to others (vs. 4 & 5):** God gives insight to understand the meaning and purpose of every situation if your relationship is right with Him. You should be right in prayer, in your life-style and in your testimony. Apostle Paul did not boast of his racial and religious pride in proclaiming his faith (2 Cor. 11:21, 22 and Phil. 3: 4-6).

Your references and your religious background are not useful for affirming faith in Christ. As in childbirth, pain and suffering, bring forth a new life to earth so also, a new life will bring suffering and pain for sustaining faith.

2. **Our faith ought to overcome trials (vs 23, 24):** Daniel's faith was tested when he was put in lion's den (vs 16). King Darius being overwhelmed by the victory of Daniel's God wrote a decree "to the people of his kingdom to fear and revere the God of Daniel" (vs. 26). Thus, Daniel's God was honoured and glorified.

Paul's faith was tested in tragedies and sufferings. He did not reckon his success as his personal triumph (2 Cor. 11:30) but gave glory to Jesus Christ in all situations.

Daniel and Paul went through physical, emotional and mental pains but never did they compromised on the issue of their faith on the living God. *Suffering and pain squeezes out dross from your faith to make you shining radiantly to lead a victorious and glorious life in Christ Jesus.*

Chapter - 4

"Lord, draw me closer to you"
(Devotional or surrendered life)

4.1 Worshipful Life

Stains on the altar of worship
Matthew 19: 16-22

There are three aspects of knowing God to realize whether you are worthy to worship God who is holy and righteous, full of glory and honour, awesome and mighty, loving and living and above all the Creator of the universe and the re-creator of your soul.

1. **Knowing God (vs. 16):** Unless you know God fully and correctly, you do not know your spiritual health and therefore you may not be worthy to worship Him. Pride and prejudices, fear, doubts and dogmas and above all rationalism make people think they are wise and holy.

   The rich young man wanted to earn righteousness by "good works". You may appear good before man and better than others but in God's sight your righteousness is filthy and your wisdom is folly. *God ought to know you and accept you as His own* (2 Tim. 2:19).

2. **Experiencing God (vs. 20):** You do not experience God by worshipping Him regularly on Sundays, by giving tithes, following and honouring all traditions of the church. Unless you experience the presence and power of Holy Spirit to glorify the name of Jesus, you are not right in your relationship to experience God.

King David pleads "Do not cast me out of your presence, O God" (Psalm 51:1). Moses pleads with God that His presence should go with him (Exodus 33:14, 15). The Spirit of God grants you wisdom and power to discern what is right and what is wrong.

3. **Obeying God (vs 21):** Jesus said, "follow me and obey my laws that lead to eternal life and do not follow the laws of sin that leads to death" (Romans 8:2). The law of the Spirit is not relative to change with time, for it is the truth and it doesn't change. You worship Him in Spirit and in truth by obedience to His commandments.

The rich young man seeking to inherit eternal life went to a "good teacher" and not to God. He followed the precepts without divine power and strength and got lost for clinging to wealth.

Stains on the altar of worship
Matt. 16: 21-26; John 16:5-15

Stains on the altar of worship are caused because of incorrect and inadequate understanding (knowledge and personal experience) of Jesus Christ. Perception of Jesus, the God incarnate, ought to be spiritually sound to worship Him free from stains. *Yet some worship God with misconception of God and also about themselves.*

1. **You ought to know Jesus as Saviour and Lord of your life:** Peter who confessed Jesus as the son of living God, denied Him three times. Peter also misunderstood the mission of Jesus (Matt. 16:22 & 23). You must understand and acknowledge that Jesus is the only person for your reconciliation with God through the shedding of His blood on the cross. With conviction as of apostle Paul, you are worthy to worship Him as your Saviour and Lord (Phil. 4:8 and 9).

2. **You ought to be sanctified by the Holy Spirit always:** A life justified ought to be purified by the transformation of your mind through the indwelling Spirit in you (John 16: 12-14) & (Romans 12:1 & 2). Your life is being sanctified by the Spirit and the Word to lead an exemplary life of Jesus. Your heart and soul are clean before God to worship Him (Matt. 5:23 & 24, Eph. 4:26).

3. **You ought to know the will and purpose of God (Matt. 16:24-26):** Unless your prayers and petitions, wishes and desires are not according to God's will and purpose; God does not answer (James 4:3). You expect miracles to happen but they do not, till you express your secret sins to God and patiently wait on Him.

God's sovereign will may cause disappointments to you, but those who cling to Him receive answer in God's time. God's promises are valid. Claim the promises of Romans 8:28 in prayer.

Stains on the altar of worship
Mark 7:1-9 & John 1:14-18

We focus again on three factors that cause stains on the altar of worship. Anyone or all of them can cause stains in your worship. Jesus said, "true worshippers should worship God in spirit and in truth" (John 4:23).

Outward show of religiosity in worship as was in Judaism or practiced presently in some local churches, is rejected by God (Mark 7: 8). When you have right relationship with God the Father and God the Son, Jesus Christ and honestly confess your unworthiness before the Holy God, you are worthy to worship Him in truth and in spirit.

1. **Concept of God (Mark 7: 1-4):** Some have wrong concept of God, they are not worthy to worship Him. If they memorize Bible verses and recite the Lord's prayer, or

say "grace" before eating meals or if they attend Sunday worship regularly they consider worthy to worship God. Such religiosity practiced by some Christians are no different than the ritualistic and legalistic practices followed by Pharisees (Matt. 19: 20 & 21).

Some attend worship to hear the message from a preacher or a pastor, to satisfy the desires of their itching ears. They look to mens' power of oration and not to God's Word. God looks at the heart of man (1 Sam. 16: 7b) and not to your outward practices and traditions.

Those who worship God must experience the presence and power of God in worship. Similar was the experience of Isaiah (Isaiah 6:5), Ezekiel (Ezekiel 1:18) and of Daniel (Daniel 10:17,18).

2. **Concept of Jesus, the God incarnate (John 1:14 & 18):** When Jesus is taken for granted, you do not know the plan of God's salvation - as to why He came to earth in human flesh and blood. Your perception of Jesus is either blurred or wrong. *You may claim that you know Jesus personally. It is not enough, for God should also know you* (2 Tim. 2:19). For you may know many great people but they may not know you. In that case, you cannot have personal relationship with God.

3. **Concept of your own self (Mark 7: 5 & 6):** Without being justified (saved) you may still worship God to inherit eternal life in heaven. You desire peace from God to lead a holy life and worship Him. The young rich man bargained for eternal life but got lost (Matt. 19:22) for his concept of Jesus and of himself did not conform to divine standards.

What in life are you bargaining for to inherit eternal life? Are they for your reputation, power and position, wealth and prosperity on earth or eternal life in heaven?

Stains on the altar of worship
Isaiah 6 :1-4; John 1:1-14: Lk. 18:9-14

Christ being made equal to many other gods and goddesses you should carefully know and understand correctly whom you worship and why you worship Him ?

1) **Incorrect assessment of God :** Our God is a jealous God and does not want any one else be worshipped besides Him (Exodus 20:3). He is a God of holiness and righteousness, splendor and beauty, purity and power, glory and honour (Isaiah 6:3). He is awesome and sovereign.

   God knows the heart of those who worship Him in truth (1 Sam 16:7b). He has established the relationship of responsibility with His chosen people with a new covenant (Heb. 10:16). He honours what He has committed. He is an unchanging God, same yesterday, today and forever (Heb. 13:8).

2) **Incorrect assessment of Christ :** He is God incarnate. He was with God in the beginning (John 1:2) and came down to earth from God in flesh and blood to dwell among us (John 1:14). The purpose for which he came to earth is to die on the cross for your salvation. When you do not know the deity of Jesus fully, you become a stumbling block in the body of Christ, the church.

3) **Incorrect assessment of Self :** The Pharisee considered himself righteous as he worshipped God in prayer, (Luke 18: 11& 12). He returned unjustified. In contrast, the tax collector's worship was justified. He prayed in humility seeking forgiveness of sin (Luke 18 :13). He asked God for grace and mercy. Matthew 5:23 and 24 tell us to reconcile with your brother (brother in Christ) before you come to the alter of worship. Worship God with your living body and not with a body dead spiritually (Rom. 12:1).

Do not worship God according to the Law of Judaism ritualistically (Jer. 6 :20-21) but worship Him with sincerity of heart (Heb. 10:16).

Our great God is worthy of worship
Psalm 90:1-17 & Deuteronomy 8:1-14

Memory is a gift of God useful for two purposes. To remember the things that are encouraging and beneficial for building spiritual life (Phil. 4:8) and secondly, to leave those things which restrict and damage spiritual life (Phil. 3:12-14). The chosen people- the Israelites remembered and practiced worship relating to rituals and traditions and ignored knowing and obeying God. God wants His people to remember three things to worship Him.

1. **Remember your Salvation (Deut. 8:1-14):** Salvation is a miracle and many forget this experience. The Israelites forgot their deliverance from the bondage of slavery in Egypt. Salvation experience is forgotten by some, some where on the way. This happens because of complacency, indifference and pride of life and also for deliberate disobedience to God's will and purpose. **Such people have everything to live with but have nothing to live for.** They forget their Creator who has recreated them in Jesus Christ as a new person. Remember your salvation as you take part at the Communion table.

2. **Remember your spiritual heritage (Psalm 90: 1&2):** Isaiah, Ezekiel, Daniel and Saul were speechless when God met them. They worshipped Him (Is.6:5; Ezk.1:28; Dan.10: 16,17; Acts 9:5). Realize your worthlessness in the light of God's holiness and righteousness. Remember the dignity of your spiritual heritage so that your worship comes up to God's standard.

3. **Remember your life on earth is vanity and limited by time (Psalm 90: 10 and 12):** Worship is a necessity. Remember what King Solomon said, "Everything on earth is vanity." Overcome the temporal things on earth such as pleasure, power, position, wealth and reputation. Set your heart and mind on things above (Col. 3:1,2) and worship God who is worthy to be worshipped. As you worship the eternal God you long for eternity.

The right way to worship God
Luke 18:9-17

Your spiritual life in relation to God's absolute standard of holiness, love and justice ought to be such that your worship is pleasing and acceptable to God. You do not have to worship your pastor nor the church leaders or preachers: for worship belongs to God.

1. **Worship God in the lowliness of heart:** Self-righteousness, pride of life and longing for power and position are from the world and not from God (1 John 2:16,17). The prayer (worship) of the Pharisee was rejected by God and he went back unjustified (Luke 18:14).

   The tax collector worshipped God with humility, confessing that he was a sinner (an unworthy person) and sought God's mercy (Luke 18:13).

   Paul confessed in his letters to the churches that he was a servant of Jesus Christ. He realized that his legalistic righteousness is nothing but rubbish in the sight of God (Phil.3: 6,8).

   Jesus, exalted God the Father, in taking the nature of a servant, humbled Himself and became obedient to death (Phil. 2: 7,8).

2. **Worship God in the likeness of "little children":** Jesus said, "The Kingdom of God belongs to little children"

(Luke 18:16). Little children without their parents have no status or no identity in society. They are socially irrelevant. They have a "clean heart", free from falsehood and hypocrisy. The Kingdom of God belongs to "nobodies" like a little child. Those who humble themselves, not boasting of status and position are relevant in God's Kingdom.

Worship God with a clean heart, without any malice towards anyone. Those who worship God with a clean heart are pleasing and acceptable to God.

Worship Him who watches over you
Psalm 8; Psalm 121

Nothing is hidden from God. He is omnipotent and omniscient. He knows everything – each one's past, present and future. He knows each one's worth (Psalm121:4). Because He is mindful and watches over each and every person (Psalm 8:4 and Psalm 121:1,2).

His chosen people ought to remember:

1. **His covenant:** A covenant is a sovereign pronouncement by which God obligated Himself a relationship of responsibility. God honours all promises given to His chosen people and to mankind at large.

   The last and the final covenant is the new covenant in the blood of Christ. He established the new covenant to deliver men from bondage of sin. He delivered Israel from exile in Babylon (Psalm 105:8 and 9) even when they failed to honour the covenant (relationship) and forgot their deliverance from Egypt (Psalm 106:21).

2. **His love and compassion:** God lavishes His love on those who are purchased by the blood of Christ (1 John 3:1). His own people in turn should pour out divine love in compassion for others so that others may know Christ and His love for them (John 13:34).

3. **His grace and mercy:** God knows that man is dust (Psalm 103:14). Man cannot save himself nor can he sustain himself in this wicked and perverse world. God grants His enabling grace and gives him the living hope of eternal life on earth and also in heaven.

So, worship God with a deep sense of gratitude and thanksgiving to God for His new covenant, His love and compassion and His grace and mercy.

4.2 Prayer Life

Counter the offensive of the devil by prayer
Gen. 32:22-30; Haba. 3:16-19; Acts 7:51-56

To counter the enemy, God had equipped us with resources. Prayerful life is one of the important resources to fight the spiritual battle against the devil. The power of the Holy Spirit is the prime resource. Without Him, other resources are ineffective to counter the attack of the devil.

Prayer has three elements.

1. **Prayer is for experiencing God :** As we pray, we lift up our eyes unto God to behold His glory and majesty. We exalt and honor His name to experience God's presence. When the presence of God is not experienced in prayer, you remain where you were before. *Pray like Jacob continually to experience God's blessing in prayer* (Gen. 32:25; 1 The. 5:17).

2. **Prayer is for receiving God's power:** This power is supernatural and comes from the Holy Spirit. Through prayer, you receive answers to many troublesome questions. Prayer becomes a joyful time. Peter and Silas prayed and sang hymns to glorify God. They were not only freed from the jail but had the power to bring the entire jailor's family to experience salvation (Acts 16: 25-

34). *Pray like Habakkuk to receive God's power of understanding* (Haba. 1:2 and 3:18 and 19).

3. **Prayer is to experience God's love :** The more you love God, the less you ask for yourself in prayer. Your degree of love for God is measured by the intensity of your prayer. *When your prayer is like Stephen, you meet God face to face* (Acts 7:55 and 56).

Victorious Praying
Matthew 6:9-15

Jesus is the author of this prayer. He is the only one who has prefect understanding of human heart. So, He can only teach the prayer that is perfect for man and pleasing and acceptable to God. For victorious living, there should be victorious praying.

Part I

1. **The prayer starts with "Our father"** not 'My father'. This brings home the most important aspect of Christian fellowship. All Christian irrespective of class, creed or colour, belong to God. He is our Father and we are all brothers and sisters. If we really believe this then only we can pray Lord's prayer. Let our relationship with God be right and also with fellow believers in Christ. Jesus said, "go to your brother and be reconciled before you come to the alter of prayer" (Matt. 6:24).

2. **"Hallowed be Thy name":** Adoring God and glorifying His name is the most significant aspect of worshipping God. The glory of God is in His name. His name is beyond human comprehension. "Jehovah" means His will is sovereign, His word is irrevocable and His purposes are sure. God's character is revealed in His name. He is the provider. He is the source of victory. He is our righteousness.

3. **"Thy Kindgom Come"**: This experience of missionary zeal and concern is for all the people of earth. A person cannot pray for the Kindgom of God to come without being saved and having right relationship with God. It has two fold meaning.

   a) *It anticipated a Kingdom of glory.* A believer's trust rests on the hope of Lord's glory. All the wickedness of human experience will cease and Satan will be bound.

   b) *It is a prayer for Kingdom of grace.* It relates to the life of a believer on earth. Kingdom of glory and kingdom of grace coexist. One has no meaning without the other. A Christian's hope is eternal glory while enjoying grace now. When we pray "Thy Kingdom come" we acknowledge that we have became citizens of this kingdom by His grace and the same grace will help those who are still outside to become His children.

4. **"Thy will be done in earth as it in heaven"**: God is our Father and believers belong to His family. Our Father has a name which we must honour. He has a kingdom to which we belong. He has a will, which we must obey.

   a) Obedience to God's will requires continuous revival and renewal by the Spirit. Continuous fellowship with God enables the believers to know God's will and His mission.

   b) Submission to God's mission requires obedience and self-denial. The total surrendered life of Jesus and His obedience to Father's will is the best example for believers. This is possible only with His enabling grace and power.

Part II

After worship, adoration, seeking God's Kingdom and submitting to His will, the focus is human need.

1. **"Give us this day our daily bread":** God provides for all human needs (Matt. 7:11; Phil. 4:19). He knows our needs. The believers in Christ must recongnise that the deepest need is Jesus Himself, "The bread of life". He provides all power and strength.

   a) The method of God's giving is implied in the petition- Give us day by day our daily bread. God provides grace on a daily basis. We cannot store two days grace for tomorrow. Daily fellowship with God, with prayers and reading of Word provides grace for daily need.

   b) God gives answers to all petitions, but all may not confirm to our desire. Acceptance of God's will is necessary to realise the adequacy of bread for both body and soul (Prov. 30 :8).

Part III

1. **"Forgive us our debts as we also have forgiven our debtors":**

   a) *Consciousness of sin against God the Father.* When God's children commit sin they break the heart of God. Asking forgiveness for the disobedience to God's will and for thoughtless action ensures experience of grace.

   b) *Confession of sin before God* (1 John 1:7-9). Consciousness of sin leads to confession. Since God had purchased all believers by His own blood, we belong to Him. We owe everything to Him. Daily confession of sin restores our fellowship with Him.

   c) *Consciousness of sin against fellowship.* Total restoration of fellowship with God takes place when we forgive others. God forgives without any limit. God enable us to forgive our brothers without limit (Matt. 18:22). The limit of being forgiven depends on the limit of one's giving forgiveness to others.

Part IV

1. **"Lead us not into temptation, but deliver us from the evil"**: The previous petitions relates to the forgiveness of past sin, this seeks divine help for the future sin. We need to experience victory over the evil one the Satan, who is constantly at war with us. The prayer is to overcome the conflict between flesh and spirit.

    a) We must realise how powerful is sin and how weak we are against it with our own strength (Rom.7:19). According to God's promise His strength is perfected in us in our weakness (2 Cor. 12:9b). Victory over sin in past does not guarantee victory over the same sin in future. The same sin may appear in a different, attractive and new grab. We are seeking deliverance from the repetition of sinning. The power of victory over the power of sin comes from God (Rom. 7 :25).

    b) We must understand the character and tactics of our enemy in the warfare. We must not hold the circumstances and situations in our lives responsible for sinning against God. God never tempts us to sin (James 1: 13-14). He permits temptation to prove our faith. In every situation, we must verify the fact with the Word of God.

2. **"Deliver us from evil"**: We live in this world in the midst of sin. We are delivered from the power of sin but not from the presence of sin. In this petition, we are seeking God's help to rescue us from the tempest that rage around us. Evil has two distinct features.

    a) *Evil that is internal.* Our own sinful nature is the strongest weapon that Satan uses against us. (Rom. 7:18-25). So we must intercede with God for the transformation of our attitude.

b) ***Evil that is external.*** As long as we live, suffering and pain are inescapable. Sometimes they are used by God to discipline us and it works for our good (Rom. 8:28). We must intercede for these according to God's will. The greatest internal enemy is physical death. However, believers are more than conquerors through Christ over this enemy as they enter the eternal glory.

Part V

1. **'Thine is the kingdom, power and glory, Amen':** By praying this, we fully subject ourselves to the King who is supreme in power and glory, and who is worthy of our praise. God demonstrates His power through:

   a) ***Written Word of God*** **(Ps. 62 :11).** The Scripture tells us power belongs to God. The Word of God in our heart keeps us from sinning against Him (Ps. 119:11).

   b) ***Renunciation.*** God became man. He renunciated His heavenly glory and took upon Him the form of a servant and humbled Himself to death on a cross (Phil. 2 :7-8). Humility is divine power.

   c) ***Resurrection.*** Resurrection of Jesus is the greatest power of God shown on earth.

   d) ***Reconciliation.*** Reconciliation of sinners with Holy God is the demonstration of God's power over sin. Regenerate people are powerful people to turn the world upside down.

2. **Amen:** The last word of the prayer is 'Amen'. All the time we utter this without understanding the meaning . 'Amen' is a name given to Jesus Christ (Rev. 3:14). By 'Amen', we seal very petition with the name of Jesus Christ and we do so on the promise of Jesus Christ (John 14:13).

Problems and Promises in Prayer
Matthew 7 : 7-11

Many people in this world pray but prayers of God's children are different. Unfortunately many Christians' prayers are neither a part nor a way of their life. As a result, their prayer is sporadic and inconsistent.

1. **Problems in Prayers :**
   a. *When prayers are limited to petitions only.* Asking, seeking and knocking are restricted to limited application. Jesus taught us prayer of adoration, confession, intercession and submission. When we pray to a holy and living God, we ought to worship and adore Him fast seeking cleansing of sin. The Psalmist says, "If we have seen sin in our heart, he will not hear" (Psalm 66 :18).
   b. *Greatest of all problems is unanswered prayers.* Moses prayed that God should allow him to enter the promised land. But God did not grant his petition. Paul prayed thrice for the thorn to be removed from his body. God answered this prayer in a different way, "My grace in sufficient for you..." (2 Cor. 12:9).

Our Lord prayed in the garden of Gethsemane seeking God's will. It was answered according to God's desire. God is sovereign and He acts according to His will and purpose in our lives. When He answers either immediately or later or even when He keeps silent, it is His prerogative.

2. **Promises in Prayers:** Problems in prayer can be overcome by looking at the promises of prayer.
   a. Jesus said, "Ask, seek, knock implying persistency in prayer. Persistent prayers look to God who is the giver of all good and perfect gifts" (James 1:18).

b. God's promises are necessary for us to claim in prayer
      i) "I will never leave you nor forsake you" (Heb. 13:5).
      ii) "My God shall meet all your needs according to his glorious riches in Christ Jesus"(Phil. 4:19).
      iii) "We are more than conquerors through Him who loved us" (Rom. 8:37) and the Scripture contains many more promises. Eyes of a believer on Christ is focussed on God in prayer than on problems only.

Jesus promised, "Seek ye first the Kingdom of God and His righteousness, and all these things shall be added unto you" (Matt. 6:33).

The Dynamics of Prayer
Luke 11:1-8

Prayer is dynamic. It is a living experience and has power in it. Jesus gives an illustration to bring home the power of prayers. This illustration brings out four truths.

1. **Relationship:** Because of relationship of friendship, the man goes to ask for bread. In order to approach God with request, one has to have relationship with Him. In John 15:14 and 15, Jesus said, "You are my friends, I do not call you servants,..." Unless we have that relationship of friendship with Him we will not enjoy that access for asking anything in prayer.

2. **Confidence:** The man goes to his friend's house at midnight. The time was unfavorable but he had full confidence that even if the door is locked the friend will respond positively. The man persistently continued to knock till the door was opened. He not only had confidence but was persistent and had patience also.

3. **To help another person:** The man is asking to meet the need of another person. Most of the time, Christians pray for their own needs. God is teaching us through this illustration to pray for others with same persistency and patience as ours. Then only our prayers can bring blessing to others.

4. **To keep the honour of the friend:** It was hard for the man who had already gone to sleep with his family to get up at mid-night to help his friend. But to honour his friend he opened the door. If Jesus is our friend (John 15:14), then in times of our desperate need and critical situation He listens to our prayer to keep our honour. If we honour Him He will surely honour us.

Remember, God answers the prayer of His children for His own honour and glory. Therefore, when we pray, our motives should be clear and concern genuine (James 4:3).

4.3 Reading the Word of God
How to read the Bible
1 Cor. 2:10-14; 2 Tim. 3:15-17

You read the Bible certainly. But do you read to study and meditate or apply your mind to the truths you read ? Please note the three precious gifts of God to mankind - His Son Jesus Christ, His church, the body of Christ and the written Word of God, the Scripture.

The truths of the Scripture are absolute, reliable, objective and authoritative (2 Timothy 3:16). So, as you study, do not try to tamper with the unchangeable truth in interpreting it. The Bible is the sole authority of our faith and doctrine. So understand clearly the power and authority of the Scripture. Read it:

1. **With the power of the Holy Spirit (1 Cor. 2:13 and 14):** The Word in the Scripture is God - breathed. So the Spirit of God alone can interpret the truths correctly. When you try to understand the Scripture with human wisdom, you fail to understand the meaning correctly.

2. **Prayerfully:** You will hear the voice of God as your heart and mind are focused on God.

3. **Lovingly:** More you love Jesus, more you will love to read the Scripture and vice-versa.

4. **Expectantly:** God's Word never returns empty without accomplishing the purpose for which it is sent (Isa. 55:11). It shields you against the devil and keeps your path in the right track of life (Psalm 119:11 and 105).

Therefore, read the Bible to be wise, believe it to be safe and practice it to be holy. Jesus said, "You are in error because you do not know the Scripture and the power of God" (Matt. 22:29).

Counter the offensive of Devil by the Word of God
Psalm 1:1-6 and 1 Cor. 2:10-14

The living Word of a living God is written in the Scripture (2 Tim. 3:16). The Bible comes alive only when the Holy Spirit is at work in your life. Otherwise, reading the Scripture becomes a routine or an academic exercise. Jesus countered the devil's temptation thrice by quoting from the Scripture and overcame the evil designs of Satan (Matt. 4:4-10).

1. **The language of the Bible is spiritual (1 Cor. 2 :11 and 13):** Many do not understand the language of the Scripture by reading it without being led by the Holy Spirit. Submit to the power of the Spirit to make your Scripture reading purposeful, powerful and meaningful.

2. **The reading of the Bible is a fulfilling experience (Psalm 1:1-3):** The meditation of the Word of God will convict and comfort, correct and enlighten, encourage and inspire to lead a holy life in Christ.
3. **The revelation of the Biblical truth gives light (Insight) (1 Cor 2:10 and 14):** God reveals the deeper meaning of the biblical truth by the Holy Spirit when you remain still in His presence with a heart of expectancy. God grants you the power to discern and insight to know which is right and what is wrong.
4. **The message of the Bible is God's love and salvation (John 3:16):** God's love is so vast that our love for Him and meditation on His Word to learn from Him is always inadequate. His love is so great that it caused miracle of salvation in our lives.

As you read and meditate on God's Word, you experience God's love to grow in the joy of salvation.

4.4 Church Life

Church is the temple of God
Matt. 16: 13-19; Eph. 2:19-22; John 2:21

Church is the temple of God and is the dwelling place of the Holy Spirit. The centrality and significance of church is Jesus.

1. **Jesus is the builder and possessor :** Jesus said, "I will build my church on this Petros" and Petra in Greek is "Rock". Based on the confession of Peter that Jesus is Christ the Son of living God (Matt. 16:16), the Church of Christ is being built on the solid, unshakable and immortal "Rock". This Rock in the Old Testament (Deut. 32:4,15,18,30,32) is a metaphor which God revealed in the New Testament in Jesus Christ .

   Jesus Christ is claiming, "I will build my church" - meaning He is the owner and possessor of the church and no one

"Lord, draw me closer to you"

else (Matt. 16:18). He has purchased the church with His own blood (Acts 20:28). The gates of hell will not prevail against it because His church has the divine power of Holy Spirit.

2. **Jesus is the foundation (1 Cor. 3:11 and 16):** No one howsoever great he may be, he is only a part of the church (God's temple) united with other believers in Christ to form the building (Eph. 2:21-22).

3. **Jesus is the cornerstone – livingstone (1 Peter 2:4-5; Eph. 2:20):** Each believer is a part of this building as a livingstone and Christ is the cornerstone. The cornerstone diffuses the attacks of the devil against the Church of Christ. Each believer may not be perfect yet they edify each other in the body to hold each other in unity and solidarity. (2 Cor. 6:16).

So, when Jesus is supreme in the church all differences and disputes are resolved by the presence and power of Holy Spirit.

Church is where God is worshipped
Malachi 1

The Scripture portion refers to a dialogue between God and His chosen people of Israel. God tells them to worship Him. Remember, worship is the jewel of Christian church. God created men and women to worship Him.

1. **Worship Him in reverence (vs. 5 and 7):** Israel offered lame and blind animals and polluted gifts to God in worship. Whereas, people were and are honored with much better gifts. Worship God in reverence, joy and peace in heart. Surely, we are receiving a Kingdom that is eternal and unshakable; "With expectancy and confidence worship Him in reverence and awe" (Heb. 12:28).

2. **Worship Him with sacrifice (vs. 8):** Are you guilty of worshipping God at your convenience of time and

situations and also do not give offerings (tithes) to Him in worship? Do you have time for personal devotion, family worship daily? Sacrifice of time and giving offerings to God generously.

3. **Worship Him with purity of motives (vs. 13&14):** When motives behind worship are not good, God is not honoured. Worship God in correct and right motive (Eph. 4:26; James 4:3).

Worship of true and living God comes first and it supersedes all other priorities in the life of all who know Him and acknowledge His greatness and love (Exo. 20:2–4; Matt.22:37).

Form and freedom of corporate worship
Gen. 4:1-7; John 4:19-24

God does not put premium on ignorance to worship Him in any way you like. When worship is not up to the standards God has set for His worship (John 4:24), He is not worshipped truly. The Spirit leads to acknowledge the truth in exalting and glorifying the name of Triune God in worship.

There are two integral parts of corporate worship— (i) Form (ii) Freedom

Truth and Spirit determine the "form" and "freedom" of worship.

1. **Form of Worship:** Transformed attitude/mind (Rom.12:2) and purified motives (James 4:3) fix the "form" of worship. God rejected ritualistic worship of the Israelites (Jer.6:20, 7:22-23; John 4:21–23). Their worship was not with genuine faith in God and was also not with purified motives. Worship is not a duty but a delight.

2. **Freedom in Worship:** The Spirit of God permits freedom in worship but determines how far to proceed. The Spirit of God limits the freedom that hinders honouring and

glorifying God in worship. Inappropriate and unholy ingredients in the order of worship lead to conflict, rivalry, confusion and division in the church. Do not recognize and honour rituals and traditions more than God in worship.

Holy Spirit grants proper balance between "form" and "freedom" so that no person but God is worshipped in reverence and awe.

Serving God in and through Christ's Body
Heb.13:7-18

Serving God in the church is practical when your faith in Christ remains unchanged with time and circumstances and you do not make commitments thoughtlessly. Inconsistency of your faith and in honoring your commitments makes you unsuitable to serve the God.

1. **Stability in faith (vs. 8):** Remember the leaders who taught the Word of God (vs. 7) and consider their ways of life and their diligent service. Imitate their unwavering faith and pursue what you receive and learn from them. Do not be carried away by all kinds of strange teachings (not related to the Bible) (vs. 9). Apostle Paul told the Corinthian Church to follow his examples to be stable in their faith in times of sufferings and trials.

2. **Stability in commitment to serve (vs. 17-18):** Obey the way leaders honoured their commitments and served. Without obedience to God and clear conscience, you can not make commitments to serve the Kingdom's cause. Jesus served God's plan of salvation in taking the nature of a servant (humility) and became obedient to death (Phil. 2 : 7-8).

When you love God, you cannot but love the church, Christ's body. When we say we love God we ought to love the spiritual leaders chosen by the leading of the Holy Spirit.

The significance of Nicene Creed and its historical background

Creed is a summary statement of Christian faith in the Triune God. The Nicene Creed came into being in 325 A.D. at Nicene, called Isnine in Turkey, when the validity of Apostles' Creed was questioned and heresies contrary to the belief of the church created confusion in the churches.

The major conflict related to Jesus, whether He was of the same nature of God or was of like nature of God and whether He co-exists with the Father. The similarity of two orders "Homousis" and "Homoiusis" with totally different meanings, caused confusion and doubt. The problem was, if Jesus is not God incarnate and is not of the same nature of the Father, we cannot be sure of the character which He reveals is the character of God necessary for the atonement of sin.

Since the heresies continued despite the Nicene Creed, another council of bishops met at Constantinople (Istanbul) in 381 A.D. and the Roman emperor officially authenticated the expression and the words in the creed for use in the churches with faith in God the Father, God the Son and God the Holy Spirit.

The Nicene Creed is under scrutiny even now but the changes are negligible and do not come in conflict with the truth of the Triune God. The Nicene Creed is a witness to our communion with the Triune God and proves the oneness of faith of all churches. It is necessary and important that every church member know the creed to believe in the faith of Triune God.

"Nicene Creed"

We believe in one God, the Father Almighty, maker of heaven and earth, of all things visible and invisible.

And in one Lord Jesus Christ the only begotten Son of God, begotten of His Father, before all worlds, God of God, Light of Light, very God of very God, begotten, not made, being of one substance with the Father; by whom all things were made : who for us and for our salvation, came down from heaven and was incarnate by the Holy Spirit of the Virgin Mary, and was made man, and was crucified also for us under Pontius Pilate; He suffered and was buried : and the third day He rose again according to the Scriptures and ascended into heaven, and is seated at the right hand of the Father: and He shall came again with glory, to judge both the living and the dead; whose kingdom shall have no end.

And we believe in the Holy Spirit, the Lord and giver of life, who proceeds from the Father and the Son : who with the Father and the Son is worshipped and glorified, who spoke by the prophets, and we believe in one holy, catholic and apostolic church, we acknowledge one baptism for the remission of sin, and we look for the resurrection of the dead, and life of the world to come. Amen.

About the Church - some instructions

1. **What is a local church?**

   It a place where:

   i) God is worshipped.

   ii) The Bible is taught.

   iii) The gospel is preached.

   iv) The ordinances are served.

   v) Christian fellowship is enjoyed and blessed and

   vi) The local church evangelises otherwise fossilises.

2. **Some instructions about attending church:**

   Pastor Norman Vincent Peale tells us how to get more out of church:

i. Go with a sense of anticipation. Have a smile ready for every one. Church should not be the place of gloom.

ii. Plan to arrive at least 15 minutes early. So that you will enter church relaxed with time for some meditation. Avoid conversation.

iii. Pray for the needs of all those round you; family, friends, strangers and the pastor.

iv. Try to eliminate any feelings you might have of criticism, ill-will or resentments. Such emotions block the flow of spiritual power.

v. Go expecting to find answer to some need of your own. Be ready to find it in the words of the hymn, the Scripture, prayer and the sermon.

vi. If it is hard to focus on God, think of a beautiful and peaceful scene of nature, how great and wonderful is His creation! To make God personal, picture Jesus looking at you with stretched hands of love and welcome.

vii. Expect something exciting to happen to your spiritual life–every Sunday morning.

3. **Obligation to attend the church:**

Hymn writer Francis Havergel says:

i. God has blessed the Lord's day (Sunday) making no exception for stormy day.

ii. For important business, rain does not keep me home and church in God's sight, very important.

iii. Bad weather—prove how much I love Christ. True love rarely fails to keep an appointment.

iv. Those who stay home from church because it's rainy frequently miss on fair Sundays also.

v. I do not know how many more Sundays God may give me. It would be poor preparation for my first Sunday in heaven to have slighted my last one in earth.

vi. I expect my pastor to be there. I would be surprised if he stayed at home because of the weather.

4.4.1 Baptism

The Doctrine of Baptism
Matthew 3 : 11-17

Baptism is not a ceremony nor a ritual nor a cleansing of the body. It is symbolic for the cleansing of the innerself reflecting the newness of life in thoughts and actions (Romans 6 :4) . This is an ordinance given to us by Jesus Christ Himself. He has set an example for us to follow.

Remember, baptism is not a means of salvation nor does it ensure eternal life. Baptism is for those who have been saved. Therefore, it is called "Believer's baptism" all other expressions used for baptism are doctrinally wrong.

1. **Baptism symbolizes cleansing by blood of Jesus Christ :** As you pass through the waters of baptism, you are dead to sin and come out alive in Christ. Cleansing by water is symbolic and relates to cleansing of innerself and not the body (Matthew 23:25-28). Without repentance and forgiveness of sin, it is not right to go through waters of baptism (Acts 2:38). It is the blood of Christ shed on the cross alone justifies true cleansing of the innerself (Roman 5 :9).

2. **Baptism is in obedience to Jesus Christ :** Jesus took baptism not to be cleansed of His sin since He had no sin. "He became sin for us so that we may have righteousness of God" (2 Cor. 5:21). Jesus justified the law of Judaism by going through the waters of baptism.

3. **Baptism leads to union with the body of Christ (1 Cor. 12 : 12-13):** You are baptised by one Spirit into one

body of Christ. It is a spiritual union with Christ and also with the believers in Christ.

4. **Baptism is necessary for receiving ordinance of Holy Communion :** As soon as Jesus was baptised the Spirit of God descended on Him signifying that He is equipped to accomplish God's plan of salvation. Those who honour both the ordinances of baptism and participate in the Holy Communion, they are useful instruments of God for witnessing Christ to the unsaved world. Through this, you fulfill the great commission of Jesus Christ.

4.4.2 Lord's Supper

The last supper of Jesus relates to Lord's Supper
Heb. 10 : 1-10; Mark 14:12-26

In His death and resurrection, Jesus made everything new. A new script of God's new covenant is written in the blood of Christ. The new covenant of the present Israel (includes all believers) underscores all other covenants which God had established with Israel (Ex. 12:14 and 17).

1. **A new covenant in the blood of Christ (Rom. 5:9; Heb. 9:22) :** The passover feast of Jesus with His disciples before He was betrayed is now the Lord's Supper as commanded by our Saviour. The last supper was celebrated in remembrance of deliverance of Israel from the bondage of slavery in Egypt to reach the promised land. So also, the Lord's Supper is celebrated in remembrance of His vicarious death on the cross for the deliverance of all believers from the bondage of sin and death to reach the land of eternal glory.

2. **A new beginning with supernatural power:** The resurrection power of Jesus Christ is our strength. Without Lord's death and resurrection, Jesus would have gone down in history as a lost case. New beginning started

with the disciples in fullness of life (John 10:10) with the power of the Holy Spirit (Acts 1:8).

3. **A new hope of eternal life:** It is a blessed hope. We await our Lord's return in glory, power and authority to receive us unto himself. His own people will be in His presence in heaven (John 14:1-4). This is the living hope of people who have living faith.

The importance of the Lord's Supper
1 Cor. 11 : 17-29

We, the believers in Christ celebrate this festival remembering our Saviour's death on the cross, His resurrection and His return to receive us. The celebration of Lord's Supper has five fold importance.

1. **It is for fellowship (vs. 17-22):** The gathering is in the unity of spirit. It signifies fellowship of togetherness among all believers transcending various denominations, culture, colour, caste and creed.

2. **It is for thanksgiving (vs. 24):** This is celebrated in thanksgiving to our Saviour for what He accomplished by reconciling the saved sinners with holy and righteous God of love, justice and peace.

3. **It is for renewal (vs. 28-29):** We cannot partake in the Lord's table without inner cleansing. Jesus brought out this truth figuratively by washing the feet of His disciples (John 13: 9 & 10). We should confess all our sins before participating at the Lord's table (1 John 1:9).

4. **It is a memorial (vs. 23-24):** We celebrate it in the memory of Jesus remembering Lord's vicarious death on the cross. This is our Lord's command.

5. **It is our living hope (vs. 26 and 1 Peter 1:3-4):** Jesus said, "Do this till I come." All believers eagerly await for our Lord's return. This is our hope.

Lord's Supper is in the memory of Jesus Christ
1 Cor. 11 : 23-29

Jesus gave us two ordinances which believers in Christ ought to honour and obey - Baptism and the Holy Communion. Jesus instituted the Lord's Supper or the Holy Communion so that His people shall celebrate to remember His death on the cross and the ransom. He has paid for us on the cross to accept us as children of the household of God.

The Lord's Supper has no inherent holiness nor it is a religious ritual. It is a celebration in remembrance, limited only to saved sinners (1 Cor. 11:27-29). The celebration has threefold meaning.

1. **It is symbolic:** In the last supper with His disciples, Jesus broke the bread and shared it with them asking them to celebrate it in the remembrance of Him. Jesus conveyed to them symbolically that His body will be broken on the cross and His blood will be shed for the remission of sins of the entire world once and for all (John 6:35 & Heb. 10:10). This also symbolically implies that our hearts should be broken to participate worthily in this memorial.

2. **It is significant:**
   i) It signifies the hope that Jesus is coming again. In participating at the table, we proclaim His glorious return corporately.
   ii) It signifies the unity of all believers that transcends all barriers human beings have created to separate people by denominations, traditions, culture, colour and race etc.
   iii) It is sacred (vs. 27-28). Sin is confessed once again for cleansing (1 John 1:9) for the celebration is sacred and holy.

4.4.3 Revival

Corporate and individual prayer is key to revival
1 Cor. 12:12–31

The church, the body of Christ, binds all worshippers together in unity which transcends caste, creed, colour and nationality. The early church set an example of corporate worship and corporate living (Acts 2:42-47). Their prayer was key to success in the spiritual and numerical growth of the church.

If you are still not a part of local church, you do not have Christian fellowship (1 Cor.12:27) to pray and worship together for revival.

1. **Corporate worship :** This shows obedience to the will of God in praise and worship, in singing hymns, in praying and studying the Word of God together. In worship, Jesus rules supreme not only in corporate life but also in individual life (Col.1:18–20). The Lordship of living God in worship make the congregation alive in faith and they renew their commitment to serve Him (Eph.5: 27 and 32).

2. **Corporate life :** Each one practices faith in unity of purpose just as a part of human body (1 Cor.12:20). Unity in a body is possible when each part loves, cares and is concerned about others well being. There is no superiority, jealousy or pride among the members (1 Cor. 3:8-9; Eph. 4:3; Rom. 12:3).

   The members of the body exercise their spiritual gifts (talents) according to the measure given to each one for unity and not for rivalry and division in the church (1 Cor. 3:3; 12:25). There is unity in their words, thoughts actions and prayer. Unity in prayer has tremendous power for revival and evangelism.

3. **Corporate living in love (1 Cor. 12:31; 13:13 and Acts**

2:44): Love is the greatest spiritual gift for corporate living. Love for each other makes the church living and healthy. *Do not long and ask for spiritual gifts according to your choice because God gives gifts just as He determines (1 Cor. 12:11).* So, pray and ask for God's love. Such love will bring revival in the church.

The body of Christ does not really grow with John and Matthew of other churches joining but when Ganesans and Sriramans become a part of the church, the body of Christ grows and becomes stronger.

Revive us again
Psalm 85 : 1-13

The Church of Christ and the followers of Christ need revival for their apathy and indifference towards God. In this Psalm, the Psalmist asks to look and consider three things for revival.

1. **Remember the past blessings (vs. 1-3):** Believers are called to remember the redeeming act of Jesus and experiences of the past days when God had proved His faithfulness. Remembrance of God's grace gives assurance for the future.

2. **Restoration of joy of salvation (vs. 4-7) :** Motive to return to God is the strongest appeal in ones spiritual life. Many times believers want God to change the circumstances or people around them, but they do not want to change and return to the fellowship of God. *Return with repentance for the restoration of joy of salvation.*

3. **Renewal for future blessings (vs. 8-13) :** Believers can expect great things to happen in the life of the church only when they are restored to God and enjoy joy and peace of God in their lives.

Revive us again
Psalm 51

Revival starts with saved sinners. It is by repairs of decay in their spiritual life. God said, "I will put my Spirit in you and you will live" (Eze. 37:14).

1. **Pardon (vs. 1-9):** David pleaded desperately to God to pardon him for the sin he committed against God and the fellow men. He confessed to God each and every sin he had committed for true repentance. His desire was to be made white as snow. Believers should not try to hide sin before God or try to please God by balancing evil with good works.

2. **Purity (vs. 10-14):** True repentance breaks the heart however God is ready to mould it again. David was seeking creation of a new heart in him. Creation is to make something new. It is not an improvement or development. God restores the heart of a believer to be new and pure.

3. **Praise (vs. 15-17):** A restored believer can sing God's praise sincerely with a clear conscience. There shall be no more guilt in his/her heart.

A restored believer is a testimony for others to bring new souls to Christ and increases the number of believers (new converts) in the Kingdom of God.

Revive us again
Psalm 51

Revival means the revitalization of decaying spiritual life. There are three stages for revival.

1. **Conviction:** Conviction of sin comes from the Word of God or from the people of God (2 Samuel 12:13). The Holy Spirit convicts us of our sins (John 16: 8). Conviction breaks the heart of a believer (vs. 1).

2. **Confession:** Conviction of sin leads to confession of sin (vs. 3). When a believer commits a sin, it is against God (vs. 4). God accepts the confession of a contrite heart and forgives and cleanses it from all unrighteousness (vs. 17).

3. **Consecration:** After reconciliation with God, the believer consecrates himself totally to God: his body, mind, intellect and emotion. Everything is committed to God through a covenant. God establishes a relationship of responsibility with you to serve Him (Eze. 22: 30a).

The Church that dares to change
Jeremiah 11:1-12

Jeremiah's message is not easy and comfortable one for the church (vs. 3 and 4). It is a message of reformation meant for both Jews and Gentiles. But for us, it is a message of transformation of mind of all members - the entire congregation (vs. 7 & 8a). Our perspective should be to build a new the church to grow from strength to strength (vs. 5).

If we think we are already strong, it may be true for us yet, it is not right in God's sight (vs. 11). Therefore, we need to submit to God for renewal with strong conviction that we accept the change whatever the Spirit tells us. We do this with determination, boldness, clarity and objectivity.

Our church should accept the rebuke and warnings lovingly and humbly and repent asking for renewal in prayer.

Three strength areas of the church which need renewal are:-

1. Teaching and practicing biblical truth.
2. Unanimity of mind in all aspects of church ministry.
3. Giving tithes and offering generously.

1. **Biblical truth :** It is not enough to learn the truth but it is essential to practice it in life. Jews were conscious of

all the covenants of God but they did not obey (Jer. 11:4). Rather, they were complacent in their worship and relationship with God (Jer. 7:4).

But Apostle Peter and Paul were obedient to God's call, they accomplished God's purpose (Acts 5:29 and 26:19-20). Knowing the truth and making it known to others brings revival.

Be obedient to truth and be opposed to apostasy (Rom. 1:21-22). Apostasy is falling away from revealed truth. It is dishonesty and spiritual bankruptcy. It is spiritual adultery (Jer. 2 : 13 & 19). The church at Laodicea suffer the wrath of God because of apostasy (Rev. 3 :16).

2. **Unanimity of mind (1 Cor. 3:1-9) :** Rivalry in the church, would strain unity of mind. Togetherness in worship and fellowship is the key to seek forgiveness and pray together to receive pardon from God for revival. Unanimity of mind is a tremendous force for revival and evangelism (Rom. 12:3 and 21, Eph. 4:3).

3. **Giving tithes and offerings generously:** When the offerings increase, it is a sign of revival and the number of worshippers also increase. Please remember if you hesitate to give to the Lord, you are robing God (Malachi 3 :8-10).

"If my people who are called by my name, will humble themselves and pray and seek my face and turn from their wicked ways, then will I hear from heaven and will forgive their sin and will heal their land" (2 Chro. 7:14).

May we claim this promise and the power of Holy Spirit shine in our lives to bring glory and honour not to us but to our God and His church.

"Arise, Shine"
Isaiah 60 : 1-4a; Matthew 5: 14-16

It is my farewell exhortation to this beloved congregation. You had responded to the challenges put across to you in the beginning of my pastoral ministry. This is a fulfilling experience. From my heart I say to you " Lift up your eyes and look about you to see what things God has done in you and in your family and what he is doing now" (Isaiah 60:4a). So arise and act. Let there be action.

1. **Light belongs to God the Creator and recreator of men :** It is the supernatural cosmic power of God which comes to those who belong to Him. Claim the power to reach out to all people of God's creation with the good news of salvation.

2. **Light must shine in good works (Matt. 5:16):** The supernatural power in you (light) should not be kept hidden (Matt. 5 :14). It should illuminate darkness and warm up people in comforting and encouraging them who are without hope and help. Do not be inactive and superactive but be active in doing good works.

Love God dearly, walk with Him closely and know Him deeply. God tells us "For I know the plans I have for you," declares the Lord, "plans to prosper you and not to harm you, plans to give you hope and a future" (Jer. 29:11).

By the grace of God, we have planted a church for the new believers and given them a pastor, three missionaries and a place of worship. Shine gloriously into the city of Calcutta. "So you become a model to all the believers... that your faith in God become known every where" (1 Thes. 1:7-8).

4.4.4 Offerings and Tithes

Grace of Giving
Mark 12:41-44; 2 Cor. 8:5

Jesus Christ taught the doctrine of "giving". Apostle Paul exhorted Corinthian Christians to give offerings to the Lord as well as for others to use. When you experience God's grace in your life, your heart prompts you to give offerings to the Lord and to His people who serve Him for the extension of God's Kingdom on earth.

1. **The primary "giving" is to the Lord (Mark 12:43-44; 2 Cor. 8:5a):** Giving tithes in the Old Testament, is according to law (Malachi 3:10).

   Presently, Christians are in the Kingdom of Grace and not in the Kingdom of Law. So we ought to give to the Lord more than what the law demands. You first offer your body as a living sacrifice to the Lord (Rom. 12:1) and give to His treasury offerings and tithes. This "giving" is open. Jesus was watching the "giving" at the temple's treasury.

2. **The other "giving" is for God's service.** This "giving" is for the extension of God's Kingdom on earth. Apostle Paul says "give to us" after fulfilling your "giving" to the Lord (2 Cor. 8:5b). Jesus taught us to give secretly to the needy (Matt. 6:1-3).

   Christians ought to realise the difference in giving to the Lord (church) and to those organisations serving God through their work.

   Do not mix "giving" to the Lord with "giving" for service. Do not confuse the mode of giving. Give secretly to His people called to serve God and the poor. This is secret.

   Remember, God loves a cheerful giver (2 Cor. 9:7).

Christian giving is stewardship
Mark 12 : 41-44

Christian giving is the result of stewardship.

1. **Why should we give?** We give to show how thankful we are to Him for all the blessings He has bestowed on us. God has given us the greatest gift of His son for our salvation and assurance of eternal life.

2. **What should we give?** How much we give is not important but the spirit in which we give matters. Macedonians gave generously out of their poverty (2 Cor. 8 : 2). They gave themselves first to the Lord (2 Cor. 8:5). Poor widow gave whatever she had out of love for Jesus (Mark 12 :41-44). But remember God wants your living body first as a perfect sacrifice to Him (Roman 12 :1).

3. **How do we give?** We should give regularly, cheerfully, generously, freely, just as 'Jesus gave Himself for us'.

4. **Where do we give?** Malachi 3 :10 says, "Bring the whole tithe into the house of the Lord." Christian organisations are engaged in the spread of the gospel and service for transformational development should be given but this giving is always over and above tithes and offerings to the Lord.

5. **When do we give?** Giving should not be governed by our circumstances. God blesses us in many ways and promises to meet all our needs (Luke 6: 38a; Phil. 4:19).

Chapter - 5

"Lord, equip me to bear fruit"
(Service in God's Kingdom on earth)

5.1 Discipleship

Discipleship in God's Gymnasium
1 Tim. 4 : 6-16

Every believer ought to be engaged in spiritual warfare to be a worthy disciple of Christ (Eph. 6:11). Therefore, every disciple need spiritual exercise to be fit spiritually and to overcome the snares of the devil (Eph. 6:13). Like physical exercise is needed to keep oneself fit so also spiritual exercise is necessary for those who are not spiritually strong (vs. 8). Spiritual exercise is needed for all disciples.

Vs. 7b – says "train yourself to be godly." Exercises for your soul in God's gymnasium is needed every day for we live in a time opposed to godly standards.

1. **God is the trainer:** There is no training without a trainer and no exercise without enrolling in a gymnasium. You need to be a saved sinner to be enrolled in God's gymnasium. You commit yourself to obey God's command and you don't rely on your own knowledge and understanding in training (Prov. 3:5 & 6). God trains you through the Holy Spirit and the Word (Eph. 6:17). The spiritual exercise is tiresome and tedious yet as a trainee you have to trust and obey the leading of the indwelling Spirit for the fitness of your soul.

2. **God's purpose of training (vs. 15-16):** This training is to make you like Christ and not to make you a pastor or an evangelist or a theologian but to equip you to be a disciple of Christ. As you are trained regularly, you grow in faith in Christ and in your commitment to serve God's cause on earth. You will be equipped to bring lost souls to the saving knowledge and grace of God.

Discipleship in God's Gymnasium
Rom. 5:1-11

What are the other conditions to qualify to enroll in God's gymnasium?

(i) You should have a right kind of life-style. Your faith should be firmly rooted in Christ (vs. 1-2).

(ii) You will have to recast your priorities in your daily life. (vs. 3-5).

(iii) You are ready to obey and follow Him (vs. 9-11).

To achieve the above, the prerequisites are :

1. **In true forgiveness of sin:** By confessing, repenting and asking God to forgive one's sin, will bring peace and joy to a guiltless heart. Thus, having the right relationship with the holy and living God (Rom. 4:7-8).

2. **In walking with Christ:** Being saved by the blood, sin will have no power (dominion) over you (Rom. 6:11 and 12). You lead a sanctified life, walking with the Lord step by step and not according to your earlier life-style thus becoming more and more like Jesus every day.

3. **In doing good works:** No, you cannot substitute or supercede following Christ by doing good works to qualify to join God's gymnasium. Abraham did good works but was justified by his faith in God (Roman 4:3; Gal. 3:9). You are saved because of your faith and not by

your good works (Eph. 2: 8-9; Titus 3 : 5-6). When you are God's workmenship created in Jesus, you do good works for which God had prepared you in advance by His eternal plan of salvation. (Eph. 2:10; 1 Cor. 2:11). You do good works by obeying and following Him.

Discipleship in God's Gymnasium - Prayer
Psalm 92:1-5

Daily Communion with God through prayer and meditation on the Word of God are important exercises in a disciples' life. Please note, your life is being sanctified every day. It is an on going process.

1. **Prayer is spiritual respiration :** One of the reasons for Christians falling short in their Christian life and life-style is their prayerlessness. When prayer life dies, the life dies a spiritual death as the flow of power from above ceases. Pray joyfully and continually (1 The. 5:16). Imitate the prayer life of Jesus (Luke 6:12 and Mark 1:35).

2. **Prayer is not optional :** Being aware that you do not continue in sin (Rom. 6:1-2), each disciple ought to pray faithfully confessing sin and seeking forgiveness always (1 John 1:9) .

   In teaching prayer to His disciples Jesus said, "When you pray." He did not make prayer optional in saying "If you pray."

3. **Prayer is an important secret (Phil 4:6-7) :** Pray for everything while giving thanks to God. Prayer accomplishes things which are beyond our understanding and expectations. God will tell you great and unsearchable things you do not know (Jer. 33:3b).

Discipleship in God's Gymnasium – Reading the Holy Bible
Psalm 119:97-112

Read and meditate on the written Word of God, the Bible. God's Word is precious and essential for building, correcting and growing as Christ's disciple (2 Tim. 3:16). Understand more clearly the power and the authority of the Scripture (Heb. 4:12).

While meditating, the mind is focussed on the living God with expectancy to hear His tender voice. It is not like transcendental meditation when the mind wanders in search of truth in the wilderness of human ideas and thoughts.

1. **Meditate effectively :** God is the author of the Scripture. (2 Tim. 3 :16). So, when you love God, you will read it lovingly and expectantly. Dr. Robert Conville says, "The more your read it, the more you love it. The more you love it, the more you read it." Reading the Bible is never a duty but a delightful exercise (Psalm 119:103).

2. **Meditate with the power of the Spirit (1 Cor. 2 : 10-14):** The language of the Scripture is spiritual. Therefore, when the Holy Spirit is at work in you, the biblical truth comes alive and is active (John 17:17). People read books for information and for reformation but Bible reading transforms your mind to be responsive to the biblical truth (Psalm 119 : 18).

3. **Meditate to realise God's will :** You hear the voice of God in mediation to know His will for you. Read and search the Scripture to be wise. You will surrender to God's will and not to your own understanding. God will make your path straight (Prov. 3 :6).

Discipleship in God's Gymnasium - Worship
Romans 10 : 14-18

A disciple of Christ ought to attend public worship to have fellowship with God and with fellow believers. A disciple ought to remain united with the body of Christ, where Triune God is honoured and worshipped in singing, praying and reading of the Scripture (Eph. 5:18-20). The essence of worship is to hear the truth as it is presented with the power and authority of the Spirit (Matt. 24:35; Heb. 4:12).

1. **Hear the reading of the Scripture (vs. 14):** Make use of the Bible, while it is being read in worship. Jesus used to open the scroll to read and people used to listen to the truth for their edification. The Old Testament tells us when the people of God heard the reading of the Scripture- the book of law, they either cried in repentance or they celebrated in joy. (2 King 22:11; Neh. 8:1-10). Faith comes from hearing the message and the message is heard through the Word of God (Rom. 10:17).

2. **Hear the teaching and preaching of the Word (vs. 17-18):** The preaching or teaching of the Word of God purifies your mind and emotions. God's Word would either convict or edify or enlighten, granting insight into deeper truths. Please note " the Word of God that comes out from God will not return empty but will accomplish what God desires in you" (Isaiah 55 :11).

Attend worship with heart open to meet God and hear His voice. "You will seek me and find me, when you seek with all your heart" (Jer. 29:13).

Discipleship in God's Gymnasium - Fellowship
Acts 2:42-47; 1 John 1:3-7

While walking with Christ, you need to be edified by fellow believers and godly people. Fellowship with God and with believers is a spiritual exercise for every disciple of Christ. It is in no-way secondary (1 John 1:7; Heb. 10:25). Do not avoid fellowship with disciples of Christ.

1. **Fellowship is for the unity of the Spirit:** The early church practiced coming together to break the bread. They ate together with gladness and sincere heart (Act. 2:46-47). Their unity of spirit helped them to respect one another in love (Eph. 4 :2-3).

2. **Fellowship is for edification – Purity:** The disciples helped and encouraged and corrected each other. They used their spiritual gifts (Rom. 12:4-8) for the common good. They cared and shared each other's burden (1 Cor. 12:25-26 and 1 Thes. 5:11).

Jesus prayed to His Father that the disciples should remain in Him in unity and in purity (John 17:11).

Discipleship is Stewardship
Luke 12:35-48; 16:1-2, 11-12

Stewardship is management of responsibility. A disciple is trained in management science to become a good steward. Jesus taught management science to His disciples to be good stewards (managers).

God, since the beginning of creation wanted men and women to be wise managers over all the resources which He had placed under their care and management (Gen. 1:27-30).

The resource referred for stewardship relate to:

i) Treasure - Money and property.

ii) Time - Setting priorities right.

iii) Talents - Spiritual gifts.

Each disciple of Christ is required to use all the resources-money, time and talent judiciously in the mission of God. If resources are misused, the Scripture tells, there is condemnation and punishment.

1. **Availability (Luke 12:35):** Availability for service is more important than ability and capability. Managing time is the essence of being available. Reset your priorities in life.

2. **Accountability (Luke 12:35):** Neglect or misuse of resources because of delay to give account to the master is punishable. Keep the finance, including property matters clean and clear.

3. **Reliability (Luke 16:11-12) :** If you are not trust – worthy, you are wasting resources. As a result, the task assigned to you is not being accomplished.

All the three qualities are essential features of a faithful and wise steward. Every disciple big or small irrespective of assignment should be faithful and be a wise steward (manager).

God's action plan for disciples' life
John 15:1-8

Three important events in the garden seem to be coincidental at human level but at the divine level, it is providential that Jesus spoke of God, the gardener and the branches are His disciples. Jesus revealed profound truth of His relationship with the Father and in interpersonal relationship with the disciples (John 15:1-8).

1. **The garden of tragedy (Gen. 2:8, 15-18) :** In the beginning, God created the perfect garden and gave Adam to look after it. But Adam forfeits the garden because of sin. The garden of Eden becomes the garden of the fall of man, a tragedy. A disciple may fall but God has plans to restore him (Joel 2:25-26).

2. **The garden of tears (Luke 21:37; 27:39)** : Jesus frequently visited the garden of Gethsemane to commune with the Father. His last visit, turns out to be a great spiritual battle field. Jesus anticipated the moment of His separation from His Father and pleads with tear. A disciple may pass through a time of sufferings and pain in his ministry.
3. **The garden of triumph (John 19:41; 20:10)** : It is the scene of resurrection and Mary's meeting with her teacher. The purpose of Jesus coming to the world makes beauty out of ugliness. Jesus speaks just one word. He calls Mary by name and she recognizes the voice of the Lord and responds, "Rabboni."

God is calling you by name and telling you "discipleship is a serious business of painful experience but in the Holy Spirit, you have righteousness, peace and joy (Rom. 14:17).

You may pray with tears but shall reap the harvest of joy.

Work and Worship
Luke 10: 38-42; John 11:17-32; 12:1-8

The three incidents relating to Martha and Mary tell us what Jesus expects from His disciples. Jesus demands priority to worship over all other means of serving Him. *It is better to be with Him in worship rather than to work for Him at the cost of worship.*

1. **Worshipping God is more important than hospitality (Luke 10:38-42):** Jesus commend Mary's action and said, "She has chosen what is better." It is better to be at the foot of the cross to worship Him and meditate on the written Word of God than doing things to honour Him.
2. **Worshipping God is important even in tragic circumstances (John 11:17-32):** Mary fell at the foot of Jesus and worshipped Him when she was full of sorrow and agony for the death of her brother Lazarus. Whereas Martha was busy narrating her sorrow to Jesus.

3. **Worshipping God is important in celebrations (John 12: 1-8):** Mary worshipped Jesus pouring out her heart to Him with deep devotion despite criticism from others when they were celebrating fellowship.

You may be busy in doing God's work but it is meaningless when you neglect worshipping Him. This is according to God's first commandment. The priority of worshipping God is so important that Jesus told whenever the gospel is preached, the life of Mary will be told in memory of her (Mark 14:9).

God's promises in your sojourn
Psalm 121

A bonafide traveller makes sure to be equipped with all travel documents, passport, visa and finance. He ought to be conversant with the culture, climate and conditions of the destination. Believers in Christ are sojourners on earth and they have embarked on a pilgrimage to reach the final destination - heaven. A passport is necessary to start the journey, to reach the destination.

By the grace of God and your faith in Christ, you have started your pilgrimage being justified but your hope of receiving the reward in heaven is not possible without being sanctified (perfected) daily.

The psalmist tells the provision God had made for the journey of the Israelites to the temple of Jerusalem. Claim these promises of God in your pilgrimage on earth.

1. **The Lord is with you in your sojourn (vs. 1-2):** The path of life is hard and cumbersome for a disciple as it was for the Israelites to climb the hill to reach the temple. They looked up to God and not to the temple for help and the help came from God. Jesus is the anchor in the pilgrimage to heaven.

2. **The Lord is watching over you (vs. 3-7)** : In the darkness of night, the Lord keeps watch over the flock. So in the dark period of your sojourn, God is mindful to protect and keep you safe. King David in Psalm 23:4 says, "I will fear no evil for you are with me." If due to some hardship, you have been backsliding, return to Him and He will lovingly restore you with blessings.

3. **The Lord is with you till the end of pilgrimage and for ever** : God's love for His chosen people is eternal. His love for them never ceases. You reach the heavenly destination if you have walked with Him faithfully. He will carry you through to the heavenly destination for He is great in His faithfulness and promises (Psalm 23 :6).

"How beautiful on the mountains are the feet of those who bring good news who proclaim peace, who bring good tidings, who proclaim salvation" (Isaiah 52:7). What is your message to your friends and neighbours of your journey to eternal home.

Having nothing yet possessing everything
2 Cor. 6:3-10

Many among us read the biography of great people to imitate them to become great. Nevertheless, if you have already accepted Jesus personally as your Saviour and Lord of your life, try Him in all circumstances - in sorrows and in pain, in need and in trails, you will be victorious even in this imperfect world (2 Cor. 6:10). It is Jesus who had nothing yet had every thing.

1. **Jesus was world renouncing yet world embracing** : Jesus said, "I am not of this world" (John 17:16), yet He so loved the world that He gave Himself on the cross for the salvation of men (2 Cor. 5: 21).

2. **Jesus was self renouncing yet self-asserting:** Jesus offered Himself as a sacrificial lamb for our salvation and did not open His mouth before the tormentors (Isaiah 53:7). But Jesus asserted with righteous anger and holy indignation at the money changers in the house of His Father for they had converted the house of prayer to a den of robbers (Matthew 21:13)

3. **Jesus was tender, yet terrible:** Jesus was full of compassion for the sinners, sick and hungry (Matt. 14:14) and instructed not to compromise even with your loved ones when it is against divine truth and purpose (Matt. 10 : 32-42)

4. **Jesus was a man of prayer and a man of action :** He prayed early in the morning to receive power from above (Mark 1:35; Luke 5:16). Therefore, all His actions accomplished divine purpose.

5.2 Fellowship

A living fellowship
Romans 12:3-13

A living fellowship is built on your living experience of salvation and your right relationship with God (vs. 4-5). This fellowship is based on two features.

1. **The essence of fellowship (vs. 6-8):** Identify your spiritual gifts and practice them for common good.
    i) Professing: Forthtale the truth without compromise.
    ii) Serving: Be a servant willing to serve.
    iii) Teaching: Interpret the Word of God honestly and faithfully.
    iv) Encouraging: Exhort and inspire one another in love.
    v) Contributing: Give to the Lord and to the needy generously and sacrificially.

vi) Leading: Lead people tenderly and diligently.

vii) Mercifully: Show mercy and compassion.

2) **The evidence of fellowship (vs. 9-13):** The manifestation of spiritual gifts are visible:
   i) Sincerity in love: Genuine (sacrificial) and sincere love is not to pamper.
   ii) Humility in behavior: Gentle and kind in conduct.
   iii) Joyful in hope: Longing for eternal glory.
   iv) Faithful in prayer: Praying unceasingly (1 The. 5:17).
   v) Caring in need: Caring and sharing for the needy.
   vi) Practicing hospitality: Home is open for healing people hungry, spiritually and physically.

Such a fellowship is a stronghold of unity and never creates crisis and rivalry (Eph. 3:6).

Fellowship ought to bring peace and joy to you
Romans 14:13-20; Ephesians 4:1-6

When every one in the fellowship accept the Lordship of Jesus Christ and each one surrenders unconditionally to the power and authority of the Scripture, there will be joy and peace, unity and purity harmony and solidarity among one another to exalt Christ in fellowship (Eph 4:3).

1. **Fellowship in Jesus name (vs. 13-14):** Jesus Christ is acknowledged as the Lord. His name is exalted and honored (1 Cor. 3:16-17). Jesus promised "where two to three gather in my name, I am there" (Matt. 18:20).

2. **Fellowship is in love (vs. 15):** A loving fellowship means sharing, caring and bearing each other's burden (Acts 2:42-43).

3. **Fellowship is friendship (vs. 19-20):** Fellowship ought to yield friendship with one another (Romans 12:3; Ephesians

4:25-26). Without mutual trust and pride in life, it is hard to befriend others. And there will be no solidarity in the fellowship. No sooner it may collapse. It is necessary to confess and forgive one another before God.

4. **Fellowship is to toil together: (vs. 19-20; 1 Cor. 3:5-9)** The fellowship thinks together, plans together and works together for the glory of God and for the extension of His kingdom.

Hindrances to fellowship
1 Cor. 12: 14–27

Poor time management, lack of love for others, lack of mutual trust and pride of life may cause difficulties to be a part of fellowship.

1. **Lack of organised life-style:** This may cause lack of time for worship and fellowship with godly people. Reset your priorities. You may be spending time in social engagements and on unproductive work. *Shape your day with the Lord and He will shape your life style pleasing to Him and to you.*

2. **Lack of mutual trust (vs. 16-19):** Fellowship is a gathering of believing people. Unless you trust and respect each other, you will not be transparent in sharing with each other your joy and your sorrows to pray together.

3. **Lack of love for one another (vs. 22-25):** Love covers (forgives) differences and conflicts in fellowship (1 Peter 4:8). Love encourages to grow in fellowship to do good deeds (Heb. 10:24-25). May the Calvary love be demonstrated in the fellowship like the good Samaritan who goes out to help neighbour.

4. **Lack of humanity and humility (vs. 26-27):** Do not think of yourself more highly than you ought but with sober judgment (Rom. 12:3). This is a hindrance to fellowship. Jesus the Master, demonstrated humility and love for

others in washing the feet of His disciples (John 13:5). Jesus "humbled Himself and became obedient to death..." to accomplish God's plan of salvation (Phil. 2:8b).

Fellowship makes you a blessing to each another and you grow in Christian life by correcting and accepting corrections.

Fellowship with God and with one another
1 John 1:3-10

When you accept Christ as your Saviour, you enter into a personal relationship with God and with fellow believers. If this fellowship breaks, it means your relationship with God and with fellow believers is under strain. This is the sign of backsliding. Sin in your life may also lead to total break down of fellowship with God and fellow believers.

This therefore needs immediate attention and correction to maintain right relationship with God and with fellow believers.

1. **Consciousness of sin (vs. 8) :** The definition of sin has changed these days. Mostly it is covered. Sin blinds your vision and understanding of God's love and the value of fellowship. Draw closer to God and you get to know the depth of sin to realise the consequences. The devil is working to break your relationship with God.

2. **Confession of sin (vs. 9) :**
    a) *Continual.* Sin should be confessed as often as needed. Be mindful that you do not fall into sin.
    b) *Complete.* Each and every sin need to be confessed. There is no small and big sin before God.
    c) *Confident.* After confession, there should be no feeling of guilt and power of sin. Jesus is our advocate who pleads before God for forgiveness of sin. Come before Him in confidence.

3. **Cleansing of sin (vs. 9):** God never forgives without cleansing. The blood of Jesus cleanses us from our sins (Rom 5:9 & 1 John 1:9). When the Holy Spirit brings to your mind, the presence of sin in your life, you should confess, seeking forgiveness and cleansing of sins immediately.

Only when the relationship with God and fellow believers is right, you have a true fruitful fellowship. *Fellowship is as essential as worship.*

5.3 Mission and Evangelism

When God Calls
1 Samuel 3

God calls to accomplish His mission through those who are free from the guilt and power of sin. The mission is one but there are many ministries (Rom. 12: 7-8).

1. **Hearing God's call :** God called young Samuel directly and not through prophet Eli. Being saved, you have a personal relationship with God. You hear God's call directly in prayer and mediation and not according to your desires or thoughts. Your ears and eyes should be sensitive to hear the voice of God. Paul received his call to mission when he was on his way to Damascus (Acts 9:15).

2. **Understanding God's call :** Samuel listened to the voice of God, understood it and responded to it. If you shrink from the responsibility to respond to the call of God to serve in the mission field and you seek "comfort zone", you are not fulfilling the plan of God.

   The disciples of Christ were with Him for 3½ years listening to His teachings. They didn't understand the mission of Christ till they received the Holy Spirit. Then they were embolden to proclaim the gospel.

3. **Obeying God's call :** Response to the call is effective and useful when you obey God's will in every step you take in your ministry. Greater is your love for Christ, greater is your obedience to God's will and commandments.

So close to God yet so far from Him
Mark 14:27-42; 66-72

During the 3½ years of ministry of Jesus, Peter among the twelve disciples had very intimate and close relationship with Him. He was with Jesus in very special occasions.

i) In the transfiguration on the mountain top (Mark 9:5).

ii) In the garden of Gethsemane for prayer before Jesus was betrayed by Judas, the Iscariot (Matt. 26:37).

iii) Disowns Christ when He was taken for trial. (vs. 66-71). This was the worst feature of Peter's discipleship to deny Christ publicly.

iv) Returns to his fishing profession even after meeting the risen Christ several times (John 21:3).

He appeared so close to Jesus yet he was far from Him. The weakness in Peter's life were:

i) Over confidence (vs. 27-31).

ii) Prayerlessness (vs. 37).

iii) Exhaustion (vs. 39-42).

iv) Isolation (vs. 66-72).

If you are too confident of your ministry, missing quiet time with the Lord, getting exhausted by overworking and neglecting your family, you are getting isolated in receiving power from God and God's enabling grace, you are far away from God.

However, Peter became an apostle after he was restored and commissioned by Jesus after a unique encounter (John 21:18) and after receiving the power of the Holy Spirit (Acts 1:8, 2:4).

God is looking for a person of His type
Ezekiel 22: 23-31; Luke 19: 5-9

God is looking for a person of His type from eternity past and was active through the Spirit to accomplish His mission. It pleased God to look for a person among Israel to respond to the invitation– fill in the gap between Him and sinful person (Eze. 22:30), but God found none. So, God sent His Son Jesus Christ to us to reconcile with those who believed in Him as Saviour.

1. **God the Father:** God looked at Adam, the first creation and through him to the entire mankind lost in sin. God found patriarchs and prophets but didn't find any one to fulfill His plan of salvation and reconciliation with God. God made a perfect plan in His Son (Gen. 3:15).

2. **God the Son:** It is Jesus, the Son of God who came down to earth to reconcile men to God. Jesus looked at Zacchaeus and through him to all who seek God in truth. Jesus came to seek and save them those who are lost. The plan of salvation which originated in eternity became a reality in Zacchaeus (Luke 19:9).

3. **God the Holy Spirit:** The Holy Spirit looked at Saul on the way to Damascus. Saul was saved from eternal condemnation and became an apostle of Jesus Christ (Acts 22:15).

Jesus is looking at you to equip you with the power of the Holy Spirit to preach the good news of salvation. Since you have received freely the gift of eternal life, share this gift freely with others through your testimony and life.

"Here am I Lord, send me" – Regenerative grace
Isaiah 6:1-8

Prophet Isaiah had an unique experience of regenerative grace. He was commissioned after an encounter with God and was equipped for the task of bringing back the fallen Israel to God.

1. **Revelation of God's splendor (vs. 4):** Isaiah beholds the glory and splendor of the awesome God in his vision. There is nothing but holiness of God all around. The seraphs worship God by saying, "Holy, Holy, Holy ! Lord God Almighty." What an experience of Isaiah!

2. **Realisation of sinful nature of men (vs. 5):** God's holiness brings realisation of man's sinfulness and unworthiness. Isaiah realises that his lips are unclean and he lives among the people of unclean lips. Even as we live in this sinful world, God wants us to live a holy life.

3. **Reassurance of salvation (vs. 6-7):** God reassures Isaiah with the "burning coal of fire". Surely, you are saved from the guilt of sin but you need to be free from the power of sin being sanctified daily. God assures Isaiah as God said to Paul, "my grace is sufficient for you." Go forth proclaim the gospel to the lost world.

4. **Response to serve God (vs. 8):** Isaiah responds saying " "Here am I Lord, send me, " he renders his unconditional service to the Lord. He did not say, "Lord send others for I have difficulties." Unless you surrender your life fully to the Lord, it will be hard to remain faithful to the great commission.

Remember Haggai 1:5-6 which says, "Give careful thought to your ways... you have planted much but have harvested little."

Your life is the fifth gospel
Romans 6:1-8

Those who are set free from sin (John 8:31-36) are slaves of righteousness of God and are alive in Christ (vs. 18). When the miracle of conversion happen in your life, you start the journey with Christ. As you walk closely with Christ, your faith gets rooted in Him and you are convinced of your faith. Your attitudes and emotions change to Christ-likeness. God who has saved us and called us to a holy life not because of anything we have done but because of His own purpose and grace (2 Tim. 1:9).

Apostle Paul claimed that his life style reflects the gospel of Christ (1 Thes. 2:8b).

1. **Conversion is not an end in itself (vs. 4):** This is the beginning of new life in Christ. It is a new life promising new values and new meanings.

2. **Conviction comes as your faith is tested (vs. 11-17):** When you overcome trials and sufferings of your faith, your faith gets perfected and becomes stronger and powerful. You are granted strength to proclaim Christ's love and grace without fear and favor.

3. **Consecration of life comes from conviction (vs. 13-14):** Your whole self – body, mind and spirit are committed with a solemn promise to serve God faithfully and honestly. You are an "altogether Christian" and your life and life style speaks the gospel- the goodness of salvation in and through Christ. You reach out to the people of all caste, creed and colour, transcending all barriers imposed by society to keep them oppressed and imprisoned in religious dogmas and poverty.

Be separate but do not get segregated
John 15:1-8

Jesus spoke to His disciples of vine and the branches to bring forth the difference between fruitful branch and an unproductive branch. In life and ministry, this fruitful branch is different in three ways.

1. **Practice holiness of life in love (vs. 4-5) :** Jesus said, "Remain in me and I in you, and you will bear much fruit, apart from me you can do nothing." You are a productive branch since all nine fruits of the Spirit is seen in you (Gal. 5:22-23). Your love and compassion for the poor, rejected and the oppressed separates you from others.

2. **Accept others as they are :** Jesus never condemned any one, not even a prostitute. When you are a branch of the vine (Jesus) you should accept them as they come and try to win them for Christ. Do not condemn them because of the difference in their understanding of the truth as you believe and practice. Rather, be a blessing to them with your Christ like life in their difficulties and problems (1 Cor. 12:7-9; Rom. 12:6-8).

3. **Listen to those who disgrace you:** A branch is not cut off immediately if unproductive but is allowed some more time to bring fruit after adequate nurturing. If you are made a fool for Christ sake, remember, you are becoming wise in Christ. You may be considered weak but you are becoming strong in Christ (1Cor. 4:10-13).

You faith and life-style makes you different that is why you are class apart from others but do not get segregated from the people around you.

How great is your God ?
Isaiah 41 : 8 -10; 1 Peter 2 : 9-12

Israel, God's chosen people (Deut. 7:6-8) had fallen short of God's plan and purpose by their disobedience to God's commandments. God sent His Son to earth to bring back him people from all nations - irrespective of whether they are Jews or Gentiles (Galatians 3:26-28, Col. 3:11; 1 Peter 2:9) because God loves all people.

God covenanted three fold relationship with His chosen people and appointed them to go and bear fruit (John 15:16).

1. **You are God's servant (Isaiah 41:8; 43:10):** It is a privilege to belong to God's family as "servant", to obey God's command which Israel failed (Isaiah 41:9). God's Son, Jesus Christ became a "servant of God" so as to obey and accomplish God's plan of salvation by dying on the cross and shedding His blood (Phil. 2:7). Do you serve this great God joyfully and willingly in the hard task of evangelisation?

2. **You are God's friend (Isaiah 41:86):** It is a great privilege to be a friend of the great God. Israel failed to be God's friend. Jesus affirmed His relationship with His disciples saying, "you are my friends" (John 15:14-15). As God's friend, we know the plan and purpose of God for you and you ought to accomplish God's plan in your life. God's plan will never harm you but has a future to prosper (Jer. 29:11).

3. **You are God's witness (Isaiah 43: 10b):** Jesus commissioned His disciples to be "my witness" (Acts 1:8). You are not your own witness. You have abilities and capabilities to glorify the great God by being His witness.

   Accomplish this task with:
   * the power of the Holy Spirit (Acts 1:8).
   * authority and clarity (Matthew 10:19-20).
   * love and humility (John 13:10; Phil. 3:8).

You are not only a witness of Jesus Christ but you are an ambassador to the unbelieving world from the Kingdom of God (Eph. 6:19; 2 Cor. 5:19-20).

You are Christ's witness
Acts 1:3-11

Jesus told His disciples that they are no ordinary people. They are extraordinary people who witness to Christ with supernatural power to accomplish a supernatural task by proclaiming the gospel of Christ to the people of all nations.

Jesus promised them that the supernatural power (Holy Spirit) would continue the work, He had started on earth. This task is going on and His people have the responsibility to continue the work with a sense of urgency.

The task is still unfinished even when the disciples had turned the "world upside down" during their ministry on earth (Acts 17:6b KJV). They had:

i) **Supernatural claim:** Jesus equipped them to reach out with the gospel to all people - starting from their homes to neighbours and to all parts of the world till the end of age.

ii) **Supernatural character:** This implied a totally new life and life-style with a transformed mind to be the same as of Christ Jesus (Phil 2:5).

iii) **Supernatural power:** This power was promised and they received Him (Holy Spirit) on the day of Pentecost. Without this power, witnessing Christ is powerless and ineffective.

iv) **Supernatural mission:** The mission is an ongoing process to expand till the Lord returns in glory. Despite all obstacles, persecution and troubles, the mission will continue.

Missionary Zeal
Acts 2: 14-41

All who are in Christ are His missionaries. *You can be a missionary only when you have a message for the people.* It is the message of salvation - good news. It tells of Christ's redemptive act on the cross and the joy of salvation.

The Scripture portion records the last words of Jesus to His disciples just before His ascension. Last words are always important. Jesus promised them the Holy Spirit which will equip them for the task but claimed their willing heart to serve with the living hope of glorious eternity.

1. **A power-filled life (Acts 2:4):** Jesus promised His disciples that the Father will send the Holy Spirit who will teach all things (John 14:26). They received Him on the day of Pentecost. This power was so fulfilling and so accomplishing that they preached and brought many souls to Christ and the first church was established at Antioch. They had no BTh, BD or DD degrees but they had the divine power of God in them.

2. **A willing heart (vs. 14):** They did not doubt even when the task was very big. They did not spend time to plan out a strategy to start their missionary work. They had the zeal to start urgently (vs. 32b).

3. **A glorious hope (Acts 1:11):** The promise that Jesus will return again in glory to receive those who belong to Him was the living hope of the disciples (1 Peter 1:3-4). They started with great zeal and vigour to win souls to Christ (vs. 38-39).

Restorative Grace
John 21 : 1-7

Peter had confessed that Jesus is the Christ, Son of the living God and was an witness to His crucifixion and resurrection, yet he forgot the mission for which he was called by Jesus. He went back to his old profession of fishing (vs. 3).

Jesus met Peter on the shore of Galilee when he and other six disciples were out for fishing.

As the story tells, the disciples along with Peter had toiled whole night but caught no fish. At the instruction of Jesus, they lowered their nets and caught such a large number of fish that their nets began to break. They must have remembered what Jesus had told them "without me you can do nothing" (John 5:5).

Jesus had an encounter with Peter. He questioned Peter thrice. Peter had denied at all three times despite his firm commitment to Jesus that he would never disown Him (Mark 14:31).

Three questions and three answers of Peter restored him to God's mission - to be a "fisher of man". This is God's restorative grace. You need three steps of preparation to be restored for God's mission.

1. **Be receptive to God's voice:** In silence God's mind moves over your mind, stimulating it to make it creative for His purpose. How much time you spend quietly everyday with the Lord?" "Be still and realise that I am God" (Psalm 46:10).

2. **Be perceptive to God's will:** Be willing to learn God's ways. Some hear but are not willing to learn. Jesus told the religious leaders, "you have ears but you do not listen or perceive what I say " (Mark 8:18). *Unless your intellect is touched by the Holy Spirit you will not listen to remember and practice.*

   When Jesus had asked Peter the same question thrice, it made him realised how serious Jesus was, while transacting with him.

3. **Be responsive to God's command :** Jesus said, "If you love me, keep my commands" (John 14 : 15). Peter surrenders fully to the command of Jesus saying, "Lord, you know everything of my life, how much I love you."

   If you do not obey God's command in your life, you are frustrating God's mission. Be receptive to listen, be perceptive to learn of Him and be responsive to follow Jesus to fulfill His mission.

Restraining grace
Acts 16:6-14; 1 Samuel 25:2-31

When God chooses you for His mission, His watchful eyes are on you so that you do not go astray but are led and guided by Him on His path of obedience and righteousness. God grants you !

1) **Sensitivity:** God's chosen person should keep his/her mind focused to understand His divine purpose, ears to listen to His voice, and eyes to see His divine purpose being fulfilled. God anointed Paul to preach the gospel to the Gentiles but the Holy Spirit restrained him from going to Asia and Bithynia, instead directed him to go to Macedonia. It is the restraining grace of God that made it possible for Paul to preach at Philippi where the first church in Europe was established after the conversion of Lydia.

   With the presence of Holy Spirit in you, you have sensitivity to move in the right direction in your mission.

2. **Self-restraint :** David was chosen by God for a particular mission and for which he was anointed as the king of Israel. God's watchful eye was on David when he came down in a rage to kill Nabal. God prepared Abigail to be the peacemaker between her husband Nabal and David. David remembered his anointing and commission which was much greater than anger leading to murder (1 Sam 25:26). God wanted that this incident of shedding blood in anger should not become a black spot in his life as king of Israel (vs. 31). The Spirit of God restrained him from doing such murderous action. Because of God's restraining grace, David honoured God in His kingdom.

God's restraining grace brings great blessing. There is no discouragement when God closes a door, He opens up another for His purpose.

A short note on "Grace of God"

Salvation is a miracle of God's grace. "By the grace of God through faith you have been saved" (Eph. 2:8). *Grace is unmerited favor for hopeless people.* It is a divine experience which gives hope of eternal life. When we were without hope, God sent His Son in the Person of Jesus to earth for the salvation of mankind.

Grace of God is connected with Christ, and our salvation and righteousness is through Jesus Christ.

Law is connected with Moses and with works of men. Under law, God commanded righteousness of men through works. Law failed to fulfill the righteous demand of blood.

Whereas, *mercy of God relates to help from God for helpless people.* God's mercy is for accomplishing a particular work.

You are Christ's ambassador
2 Cor. 5 : 16-21

An ambassador is the official representative of a country or a nation to another country. It is a highly prestigious position. But Apostle Paul says, "I am an ambassador in chains" (Eph. 6:20). This implies that he suffered and was chained for being Christ's ambassador.

Having been recreated anew in Christ (vs.17), we are "saints" in the sight of God; we are "servants of God" in relation to our fellow believers and we are "Christ's ambassador" to the unbelieving world to bring those who are lost. The ministry of the ambassador of Christ is reconciliation of sinful man and righteous God.

1. **An ambassador is appointed by the president of the country:** Our appointment is by Jesus Christ and not by

any person or organisation (2 Cor. 5:18-20). But we ought to qualify for holding such a high position in the Kingdom of God.

2. **An ambassador belongs to his own country for citizenship:** You belong to a holy nation (1 Peter 2 :9) and your citizenship is in heaven (Phil 3:20; Eph. 2 :19). You are now in transit on earth.

3. **An ambassador does not build any thing for himself in a different country:** Being ambassador of Christ, you should not work with a motive of building things for yourself on earth (2 Cor. 5:15 b).

4. **An ambassador receives supplies and instructions from his own country:** You should be led by the Holy Spirit to serve the cause of Christ on earth filled with the mighty power of God from above to counter the attack of Satan (Eph. 6:10-11).

5. **An ambassador is rewarded by his country for the "good work" he does in another country:** So also, those who serve God in this world faithfully and suffer, they will be rewarded adequately in heaven according to the promises of God (Rev. 22:12).

6. **An ambassador faithfully confirms to his own country's standards in a foreign country:** Likewise, as Christ's ambassador, you ought to represent Christ truly with Christ like attitude (Phil. 2:5) and the truth of the Scripture faithfully and correctly to others.

7. **An ambassador if insulted in a foreign land, is called back home to be honoured:** Jesus said in John 16:33, "I have told you these things, so that in me you may have peace. In this world you will have trouble, but take heart, I have overcome the world" and will have the right to sit with me on my throne (Rev. 3:21).

Christ in all and is in all
Galatians 1 : 6-17

Theology is the systematic study of the nature of God. Theology tells that God is sovereign and absolute, Creator of the universe and recreator of man. Whereas, philosophy is the study of reality that leads to rationalised thinking. Rationalism relates to relative only and not to absolute. Therefore, study of philosophy will not give the full knowledge of God.

The Scripture tells that it is through the Spirit of God we can know God truly. Jesus claimed "I am the way and the truth and the life. No one comes to the Father but by me" (John 14:6).

1. **Call of God to His people to return to Him (vs. 6-7):** God revealed Himself in His Son Jesus Christ, the Saviour of the world. He can be found when you seek Him truly and diligently (Isaiah 55:6-7; Jer. 29:13) . As of today, even His own people are still searching God in darkness and in wilderness.

2. **Compassion of God for Gnostic philosophers (vs. 14-16):** Human tendency is to rationalise to understand the mystery of God. Therefore, God's plan of salvation is not understood by logic and philosophy (1 Cor. 1:25-31).

3. **Confidence in God's promises – His covenant (vs. 10-13):** Power and authority of God is unsearchable and beyond human wisdom. What God wants He accomplishes. God is sovereign and absolute. When you know God and committed to His mission you can accomplish His purpose being co-worker with Jesus.

May the Lord equip you to proclaim Christ in all as He is in all (Col.3:11).

No rationalism and relativity can bring out God's absolute truth.

Evangelisation demands your body, mind and soul
Matthew 9:35 – 10:20

It is incorrect to think that evangelism is only to proclaim Christ. But the task is so challenging and so hard, it demands your total self. Jesus commissioned His disciples to the task and sent them out encouraging them to overcome difficulties and even rejection when they meet people.

1. **Commission is great (Matthew 10: 1)**: Jesus commissioned Peter in an unique encounter (John 21:17). Peter was equipped with power to proclaim the gospel to all the people (Acts 2:22, 37-38). You too need an encounter with God to be commissioned and receive power from above.

2. **Compelling task (Matthew 9:37-38):** The task is compelling to proclaim the gospel to the end of the earth. It is possible only through the power and guidance of the Holy Spirit (Acts 1:8) and not through human wisdom and strength.

3. **Cost is great (Matthew 10: 5-8, 16):** You have to give yourself fully to the task even when the cost you pay is very high. But your reward in heaven is great. Remember, Jesus has given His life for your salvation. How much can you give?

4. **Cast off worldly values (Matt. 10:9-10)** : Worldly things such as popularity and prosperity, wealth and comfort will cause hindrance in fulfilling God's mission. Cast them off with full assurance of receiving the glory and honour when Christ is revealed (1 Peter 1:5-7).

5. **Compassion is the key to present the gospel (Matt. 9:36)** : Jesus had compassion on people to proclaim the gospel. *Like wise, with love and compassion, authority and clarity present the gospel to your neighbours.*

Chapter – 6

"Lord, make my life a miracle"
(Sanctified life or holiness in Life)

6.1 Christian maturity – life in all its fullness
Life in all its fullness
Acts 6:1-15

Life of Stephen is an example of a life in all its fullness.

1. **Full of faith and the Holy Spirit (vs. 5):** Faith in Christ is the basis for a life in all its spiritual manifestation. This is what the "Heroes of faith" of the Old Testament were commended for (Heb. 11:1ff). The power of the Holy Spirit brings out the application of faith showing transformation in a person's life and influences friends and neighbours.

2. **Full of faith and power (vs. 8):** Faith in God grants your spiritual power to overcome persecution and trials joyfully. Stephen had the emboldening power to stand firm before the religious leaders and preached the gospel of Christ to them. He became the first martyr for the gospel.

3. **Full of Spirit and wisdom (vs. 10):** Spiritual power and divine wisdom come from the Holy Spirit. Many Christians lead powerless life without the Spirit dwelling in them. It may be a comfortable life but it is not a victorious living. Prayer and passion for the Savior humbled Stephen to patiently bear suffering to death (Acts 7:57-60).

You cannot receive the anointing unless you continue to rest in the Lord patiently to experience the glory of God in your life.

John Wesley wrote this hymn having an amazing experience of anointing-

> *"Finish then, Thy new creation*
> *Pure and spotless let us be,*
> *Let us see Thy great salvation,*
> *perfectly rested in Thee.*
> *Changed from glory in to glory till*
> *in heaven we take our place.*
> *Till we cast our crown before*
> *Thee, lost in wonder, love and praise."*

Wesley described this experience saying, *"I am now an Altogether Christian."*

The secret of positive thinking
Phil 4:10-20; 2 Tim. 6:6-10

Many have been blessed by the book *"Power of positive thinking"* without fully realising the reality of the person from whom this power flows. The Holy Spirit transforms your attitude to be like Jesus' (Phil. 2:5). With a changed life-style, you tend to reveal the fruit of the Spirit in your life (Gal. 5:22-23).

1. **Contentment (vs. 11-12):** It is not material gain that brings contentment. *It is peace with God (salvation experience) and peace from God (sanctified life) bring contentment in life.* This is the gift of divine grace. As apostle Paul said, "My God will meet all my needs according to His glorious riches in Christ Jesus" (vs. 19). Paul instructed Timothy saying, "godliness with contentment is great gain" (1 Tim 6:6).

2. **Concern (vs. 10):** As you grow into maturity, you get more and more concerned about the well-being of others – your neighbours (Luke 10:33-36). The Church at Philippi was spiritually rich but not materially. Yet, they were concerned about Paul and his co-works for the spread of the gospel of Christ.

3. **Compassion:** The Church at Philippi was compassionate towards those who worked to the spread of God's Kingdom (vs. 17). They knew that to give for a spiritual cause is better than to receive (Acts 20:35). They were positive in their thinking for they knew that it is a divine formula (vs. 19).

Jesus had compassion for the crowd as they were spiritually hungry like sheep without a shepherd (Mark 6:34). Jesus said to His disciples, "The harvest is plentiful but the workers are few" (Matthew 9:36-37).

Jesus had compassion for those who had nothing to eat (Matthew 15:32). He cared for them and fed them with loaves and fish.

As you grow into maturity, you will be content with what God has provided for you and your family. You have concern and compassion for your neighbours who are in need of spiritual and physical food.

When Jesus is the Lord of your life
James 1:9-24

Faith in Christ and good works (Eph. 2:10) are integral. When faith is genuine and real, it is seen in good works. The Scripture portion tells us of three ways to grow into maturity.

1. **Practicing faith:** Your faith is proved by your "good works" (Matt. 5:19). God's workmanship in you is visible to the outside world (Eph. 2:10). You grow to maturity with power to discern – what to do and when and when to do; what to say and what not to say and when to keep silence. Overcoming such trials of faith assures reward (James 1:12) and glory in heaven (1 Peter 1:6-7).

   "Let us run the (spiritual) race that is marked out for us to reach the goal fixing our eyes on Jesus, the author and perfecter of our faith" (Hebrew 12:2-3).

Cultivate your faith to enjoy a victorious living on earth and a glorious life in heaven.

2. **Practicing victory:** When the Spirit is subdued by the desires of flesh, temptation overpowers. Your faith became ineffective (James 1:13-15). There is victory over sin and temptation when the Word of God is in your heart (Psalm 119:11). Jesus overcame temptations by the Word of God even when he was physically weak (Matthew 4:7-10). You can also be a victor and not a victim with the Word of God stored in your heart (Heb. 10:16).

3. **Practicing humility (James 1:9-10):** Humility is not inferiority or timidity. Since there is no difference among Christians of caste, creed or race (Col. 3:11; Gal. 3:26; Eph. 3:6), there should be no pride or superiority of any one or anything. All are one in Christ under the Lordship of Jesus. Please note, the humble receive the grace of God whereas God opposes the proud (1 Peter 5:5 b).

Never-ever underestimate the power of Satan
1 Peter 5:8-10; Matt. 4:1-11

Sin enters in a very subtle way to overpower you even when you recognise that you are right in your relationship with God. When your relationship is under strain or broken with God and with fellow believers, the devil attempts to alienate you from God. Sin is committed in words, thoughts and deeds either privately or publicly.

The Scripture warns believers to be careful to deal with the snare of the devil. Satan dared to tempt our Lord Jesus Christ when He was fasting and praying for 40 days.

1. **Motivational sin (Acts 5:3-4):** Evil motives come out of lust for power, position and wealth. Submit your "good plans and programmes" to God in prayer. He will correct your motive if it is not right.

2. **Emotional sin (Gen. 25:32-33):** Many activities are for your emotional satisfaction. Esau was thoughtless in selling his birth right.
3. **Secret sin (Gen. 4:8-10):** Sin committed in secret is exposed, sooner or later. Jacob became aware of the sin committed by his sons much later. Ananias and Sapphira's secret sin was exposed very soon (Acts 5:1-10).
4. **Reluctant sin (Judges 16:16-17):** Under nagging circumstances, Samson did give into the desires of Delilah. Do you compromise to avoid nagging and commit sin reluctantly ?
5. **Positional sin (Matthew 14:6-10):** Pride in having authority and power over people may tempt you to take a sinful decision. This will happen to you if you are not submissive to the spiritual power of discernment. Herod, the king made a sinful commitment to allow the execution of John the Baptist.

Is your home a heaven on earth?
1 Peter 3:1-7

A Christian home ought to be like heaven on earth. In such a home, God is loved, honored and glorified by the parents and the children (Psalm 127; 128). Every member of such family reflect the fullness of life in Christ in and through their lives (John 10:10).

1. **Parents:** They set standards in their home under the guidance and authority of the Holy Spirit. The husband in obedience to God's commandments leads the family to worship and know the Scripture. Wife is the fruitful vine within the home (Psalm 128:3). She establishes traditions and practices in love and care for all family members. *A family that prays together and stays together and is united in love.

2. **Parent-child relationship:** This relationship is based on biblical principles (Col. 3:20-21). The parents teach their children the Word of God faithfully (Deut. 6:4-9). The parents set examples in confessing their failures and seek forgiveness at the foot of the cross daily. Such parents discipline their children without difficulty (Eph. 6:4) and their children become example in the school and church.

A family that goes hand in hand with God in all circumstances is a blessed home.

* *Please read the " Beatitudes for women " that follows.*

Beatitudes for women

Blessed *is she whose daily tasks are a labour of love; for her willing hands and happy heart translate duty into privilege and her labour became a service to God and all mankind.*

Blessed *is she who opens the door to welcome both stranger and well-loved friends; for gracious hospitality is a test of brotherly love.*

Blessed *is she who mends stockings and toys and broken hearts; for her understanding is a balm to humanity.*

Blessed *is she who scours and scrubs; for well she knows that cleanliness is one expression of Godliness.*

Blessed *is she when children love; for the love of a child is more to be valued than fortune or fame.*

Blessed *is she who sings at her work; for music lightens the heaviest load and brightens the dullest chore.*

Blessed *is she who dusts away doubt and fear and sweeps out the cobwebs of confusion; for her faith will triumph over all adversity.*

Blessed *is she who serves every meal with laughter and smiles; for her bouyancy of spirit is an aid to mental and physical digestion.*

Blessed is she who preserves the sanctity of Christian home; for her's is a sacred trust that crowns her with dignity.

Author unknown.

Every investment may not yield return
Eccl. 11:1–9

King Solomon looked around and found that every thing is vanity. For every investment, there may not be any return. Nothing, absolutely nothing can bring complete satisfaction because we are ignorant about many things, which are beyond our understanding and expectations.

Therefore, believers must strive to obey God's will and purpose because there is help (vs. 1).

1. **You do not know what evil will come upon earth (vs. 2):** The most powerful country did not know of the disaster of September 11 nor did South East Asia knew that tsumani of Dec. 26 would wipe away thousands of lives from the face of the earth (Ref. updated). Man is still ignorant of various types of disasters and natural calamities and nuclear catastrophe that might take them unawares.

2. **You do not know the works of God (vs. 5):** Man could never ever understand how God gives life to the things He has created. But God can do wonders. He has divine purpose behind every action. It is, therefore essential to make every effort to do the work well and at the earliest of opportunities, leaving the results to the Lord.

3. **You do not know what God will make to prosper (vs. 6):** Sow the seeds knowing that God is capable of producing rich harvest.

4. **You do not know what you will receive on judgment day (vs. 9):** Every deed done on earth will be judged.

Time and opportunities available should not be wasted on mortal things which perishes but store imperishable things in heaven.

Be wise in making investment in heaven where moth and rust do not destroy and where thieves do not break in and steal (Matthew 6:19).

Holy life and holy living

We ought to know that we belong to the family of holy God. Therefore, we ought to be true to the holiness of God and also to ourselves as children of the holy family (1 Peter1:15-16).

Reflection from the lives of Joseph, King David, Daniel, Queen Esther and apostle Peter will help us to strive to live holy life with the power of the Holy Spirit.

1. **Joseph (Gen. 39:5-10, 21-23; 41:41-43):** He occupied a high position in Egypt, a foreign land but remained true to his God and true to himself in the midst of every opportunity to commit sin. In all situations, *Joseph's godly life brought the best in him.* He remained pure against threat to his life. God blessed him and he prospered in Egypt.

2. **King David (Psalm 51):** *Satan succeeded in bringing out the worst in David.* When prophet Nathan told David about the sin of adultery and murder he had committed, he owned his sin, confessed and repented. God accepts a contrite and a broken spirit. He remained true to himself because he was true to God. He was a man according to "God's own heart".

3. **Daniel (Daniel 6:3-4, 19-23, 25-27):** He excelled in his prayer life in a foreign land. There was no corruption in him. Satan tested him but he remained unshakable in his faith even in the lion's den. Victory of Daniel is the victory of the living God. *He remained true to God and true to himself.*

King Darius and all the people of his kingdom came to know the living God of Daniel.

4. **Queen Esther (Esther 4:12-17; 8:16-17):** She, a Jew, ignored the threat to her life to save the lives of the chosen people of God, the Jews in Persia. She met king Xerxes to tell the king of the evil designs of Haman to massacre the Jews. Esther fasted and prayed and remained faithful to her God. Her prayer was answered. Haman was hanged instead. The Jewish community in Persia was not only protected but they also prospered.

5. **Apostle Peter (Acts. 4:8-20):** He knew who Jesus was, the Son of living God - the Messiah (Matthew 16:16) yet he denied Jesus thrice. After Pentecost, he was empowered by the Holy Spirit to remain true and faithful to Jesus in his trial before the Sanhedrin, declaring that he will testify of what he has seen in Jesus and what he has heard from Him (vs. 20). Peter is one of the apostles who "turned the world upside down" to fulfil what Jesus had asked the disciples to accomplish (Acts 17:6b KJV).

The world is looking for such holy life among the Christians. If you are true to God and honest to yourself, your life is worthy to glorify God.

You are a branch in the tree of life
John 15:1-12

Christ claims newness in your life and life-style so that you grow into Christ-likeness. Jesus gives the illustration of a vine and the branches, signifying that Jesus is the vine, the believers are the branches and God, the Father is the gardener. The key to this truth is fourfold:

1. **To bear fruit (vs. 2-3):** Bearing fruit means to bring forth the fruit of the Spirit in life. It is Christ like life and you are effective in bringing sheaves of harvest. A branch is

pruned to yield more fruit so also you will have to undergo sufferings and trial of faith in your life to bring more souls to Christ.

2. **To abide in Christ (vs. 4):** To be an effective witness for Christ, you should walk with Him closely and love to worship Him and have communion with Him in prayer and study of God's Word diligently.

3. **To obey Christ (vs. 10):** When you abide in Christ, you obey His commandments and accept His Lordship in your life. When you obey Christ, your life is being sanctified.

4. **To love God (vs. 9-12):** You should love God very dearly, honor and exalt His name at all times and at all circumstances, ceasing all opportunities (Eph. 5:15-17). This is self – sacrificing divine love which will attract people of the unbelieving world to Christ.

The last word in Christ-likeness or Christian maturity is divine love – self-giving love.

Beautiful attitudes of Christians
Matthew 5:13-16

Beatitudes relate to Christian's counter culture. As a fish swims against the stream so does a Christian thinks and acts against the thoughts and actions of natural man.

Jesus preached saying, "You are –

i) the Salt of the earth"

ii) and the Light of the world."

You are already salt ready for use by all the people of this earth. You are already light to shine wherever there is darkness.

Being salt, be useful to everyone on earth and being light be useful by shining all over the cosmic world of God. Light belongs to God.

1. **You are Salt:**
   - *i) Salt has intrinsic value in its saltiness.* Likewise as a Christian, you have Christ-like attitude for useful in church and in society at large.
   - *ii) Salt permeates.* It permeates into food to make it tasty. Christians should be a blessing to their neighbours in their service of love.
   - *iii) Salt means faithfulness.* Salt preserves food. As a Christian, you should be faithful to God in your commitments and obedience. You should not backslide.
   - *iv) Salt is powdered, refined and iodized.* Unless a Christian faces trials and sufferings for his/her faith, he/she is not suitable for God's Kingdom.

2. **You are Light:**

Light is the dawn of first creation. God said, "Let there be light, there was light." *Jesus the Son of God is the dawn of new creation.* He is the source of eternal life. Jesus said, "I am the light of the world" (John 8:12). He also said, "You are the light of the world" (Matthew 5:14).

Light shines not for reflection but for transformation and drives away darkness of guilt and power of sin. When light shines in and through you, *your labour of love and work of faith glorify your heavenly Father* (Matt. 5:16).

Finally, your attitude should be the same as that of Jesus (Phil. 2:5) to be the salt of the earth and the light of the world.

Demolish something and discipline other things
Romans 7:21-8:4; 2 Cor. 10:5

Justification is the beginning of your Christian journey and not an end. *You are now engaged in a spiritual warfare not against sin but against sinful nature.* In this struggle, you need to demolish something and discipline other things. As you discipline with the divine power of God, the demolition of other things automatically follows. Both are painful and you need God's power, wisdom and strength.

1. **Things to be disciplined:** As you start the process of disciplining yourself to be Christ-like, you:
   i) Accept the truth of the written Word of God.
   ii) Apply the truth in daily life and living.

   i) Accept the Word of God. John Scott has written "Those who reject the reality and authority of the Scripture (Bible) do not go very far in Christian life. They are stagnant and they stink. Their academic knowledge make them clever fools." Accept the authority and voracity of the Word. Jesus resisted the devil with the help of God's Word.

   ii) Apply the Word in life. Application of truth in life needs transformation of mind and purification of emotions (Rom. 12:2). Your mind is transformed to be like the mind of Jesus.

2. **Things to be demolished totally :** In disciplining your life, you have to demolish or root out something totally. These things are from the devil, he is cleverly hiding them in you. The pride of life, prejudices, religious dogmas and superstitions, hypocrisy etc. All these have to be thrown out with the power and authority of the Spirit in you. God grants you the enabling grace as you sincerely and honestly pray to God for help.

   The Holy Spirit needs to purify your emotions also. We need not completely do away with emotions and culture. They need purification to be right. We should therefore, be careful while demolishing such things of emotion and culture which are at conflict with the scriptural truth.

Apostle Paul took this struggle and conflict in his life while demolishing the things that were from the devil. In Romans 7:24, he says, "What a wretched man I am! Who will rescue me from this body of death." Praise God that he found the answer in Jesus Christ to overcome (Rom. 7:25).

Our struggle against sinful nature is nothing compared to the crown of righteousness which we will receive that day (2 Tim. 4:8).

Vices to die to live with virtues
Col. 3:1-17

When you die to rise with Christ, your life is hidden in Christ. Apostle Paul said, "I have been crucified with Christ and I no longer live, but Christ lives in me. The life I live in the body, I live by faith in the Son of God" (Gal. 2:20).

1. **Right with God:** In vs. 7 to Colossian Christians, Paul says, "you had six vices in you (vs. 5) in you before you came to know Christ, and you still have another six vices even now (vs. 8) which you should get rid off." These six are uncontrolled and unpurified emotions. Then only your life will be right with God.

2. **Right in all virtues:** All vices have to go out of life to give place to six virtues (vs. 12-13). Love is the cover garment of all virtues and binds you and believers in perfect unity (vs. 14).

3. **Right with all believers (vs. 11):** Right relationship with God and the love of God in you supercedes all differences of background of race and nationality of all believers. It is Christ who ought to rule supreme in fellowship and worship.

4. **Right in words, thoughts and deeds :** Christ shines through your words, thoughts and deeds. Equip yourself with:

i) **Peace of Christ (vs. 15).** The peace of Christ transcends all human understandings with the wisdom from God. It protects and comforts your heart and soul.

ii) **Word of Christ (vs. 16).** The Word of God prevents you from committing sin (Psalm 119:11) and is a light for your path (Psalm 119:105).

iii) **Name of Christ (vs.17).** His name is above every name. It is above all the names of people who have come and gone or those who are yet to come in human history. In His name, there is victory (1 Sam.17:45b-50). In His name, there is power (John 17:11).

"Blessed is the man who trusts in the Lord, whose confidence is in Him. He will be like a tree planted by the water that sends out its roots by the stream. It does not fear when heat comes; its leaves are always green. It has no worries in a year of drought and never fails to bear fruit" (Jer. 17:7-8). *This is fullness of life.*

Chapter -7

"Lord, help me to proclaim Jesus as the Lord in all celebrations"

7.1 Christmas

The reality of Christmas
John 1:1-14; 3:16

Many Christians and people of other faiths celebrate Christmas giving pre-eminence to Santa Claus, Christmas tree, Christmas cake and Christmas card. The reality of Jesus and the birth of Jesus- God incarnate in human flesh as a person is overshadowed. Unfortunately, the pagan practices have assumed such pre-eminence that usually the people of other faiths do not know that Christmas relates to the birth of Jesus.

1. **His birth in history:** *Jesus did not emerge out of human history but was born into history.* He came to this world from outside (John 1:13), which was prophesied hundreds of years ago before His birth (Isaiah 7: 14; Zechariah 9:9). His birth was not an accident but was according to divine plan of salvation (John 3:16). The name Jesus means "He shall save His people" (Matt. 1: 21) reveals His purpose of coming down to earth.

2. **His birth in flesh:** The word that was with God became flesh and dwelt among us (John 1:14). He became the perfect vehicle of communication between God and man. Man could understand God's love, His might, His power and authority in a personal way through the presence of the Holy Spirit. Jesus was transformed into our image so that we might be transformed into His.

"Lord, help me to proclaim Jesus as the Lord ...."

3. **His birth in us:** The word must become "flesh" in us to celebrate Christmas meaningfully. Unless Jesus is born in your heart, celebration of His birth is meaningless.

Jesus is the greatest contemporary who cannot be forgotten and ignored by anyone. Do not exclude the Person of Jesus this Christmas. May the star of Christmas guide you and enable you to walk in the light.

The truth of Christ in Christmas
Isaiah 9:2, 6-7, Matthew 1:20-23

Most people including some Christians celebrate Christmas excluding the Person of Christ. Christ is excluded in Christmas by substituting Christ by "X", thus Christmas is called X-mas. The celebration means x-haustive preparations, x-tensive shopping, x-treme decorations, x-citing parties, x-cessive feasting, x-travagent gifts and above all x-halting Santa Claus, and x-cluding Christ.

Some Christian celebrate Christmas in *carols, cards* and *cakes* only. They are happy with three C's for celebrating the 4th C - *Christmas.*

Some Christians and others celebrate Christmas in a grand party without knowing the reason why they celebrate.

His birth is still a mystery to many but three truths unfold the ministry. His birth is unique and will never happen again in human history.

1. **In Him is peace and joy (Luke 2:10, 14):** Announcement of peace and joy at the birth of a child was fulfilled in the life of Jesus. Prophet Isaiah prophesied about six hundred years before the birth of Jesus and called Him "Prince of peace" (Isaiah 9:6). Jesus said, "Peace I leave with you, my peace I give you, I don't give as the world gives." *A peaceful heart is a joyful heart.*

If you have any resentment and bitterness in your heart against anyone, you will not enjoy the blessedness of peace that come with Christmas.

2. **In Him is salvation and eternal life (Jer. 10:10a):** Jesus always claimed that in Him is eternal life (John 6:27, 54; 10:28). Eternal life promised in the Old Testament became a reality in Jesus. The name Jesus signifies salvation, which assures eternal life (1 John 4:14; 5:11).

3. **In Him is the hope of glorious life in heaven:** The hope of glorious life with Christ in heaven became real in His death on the cross and His resurrection from the grave. In His earthly ministry, Jesus proclaimed this truth to His disciples, (John 14:1-4). Apostle John realized this truth in His vision in Patmos (Rev. 7:9-10).

Jesus is Immanuel, God with us all the time both on earth and in heaven.

Do not bargain your faith to celebrate Christmas; instead remain sensitive to present Christ to the multicultural multireligious and pluralistic society with your testimony. In doing so, do not get segregated in celebrating Christmas.

Is Christmas truly wonderful?
Isaiah 8:22- 9:7

Wonderful things do happen and do not remain wonderful all the time. Jesus is wonderful all the time- wonderful before His birth, wonderful in His birth at Bethlehem and wonderful in His resurrection from the grave. He was and is wonderful in grace, mercy and love. Above all, He is a wonderful Saviour. When He comes again (Acts 1:11), He is wonderful and glorious in justice, authority and power.

1. **Wonderful in the prophecy (vs. 2-3):** God had planned from eternity past to restore the people who are lost in sin, (Gen. 3:15) through His begotten Son Jesus the

Messiah. Jesus is the anointed one of the righteous and holy God. Prophet Isaiah said, "He is the light of the world and the prince of peace." Truly, Jesus claimed that He is the light and peace (John 8:12-16).

2. **Wonderful in His birth:** A heavenly child (Jesus) was born to an earthly mother Mary (Matt. 1:21). She conceived Him by the Holy Spirit (Matt.1:20). It is a miracle of miracles and a wonder of wonders (Isaiah 7:14).

3. **Wonderful in His ministry (vs. 6):** He was a wonderful counselor. His exemplary life, His love and compassion for the poor and the oppressed (Luke 4:18), His humility and obedience to God's will and His sinless perfection were wonderful. It is so wonderful to us that He is with us – Immanuel (Isaiah 7:9; Matthew 2:23).

4. **Wonderful in His name:** Jesus promised, " Father will give you whatever you ask in my name" (John 16:23b). It is a name above every name – "every tongue will confess that Jesus Christ is Lord" (Philippians 2:10-11). In the name of Jesus, there is salvation (Acts 4:1). In this name, there is victory (John 14:13-14; 16:24). "Jesus" is a matchless name !

Christ must be formed (grow) in you (Gal. 4:19b) every year to experience that He is wonderful. Otherwise, you are celebrating Christmas keeping Jesus still a babe and He is not growing in you.

Does Christmas make a difference to you in your lifestyle every year?

Jesus, the God incarnate
John 1:1-14

God revealed Himself in Jesus, a perfect vehicle of God to make mankind know what God is like. This revelation is still a mystery to some and it is a marvel in human history indeed.

1. **His unique birth:** Jesus was born of a virgin according to the prophecy of Isaiah about six hundred years before His birth (Isaiah 7:14). This prophecy became true and real when He was born to Mary (Matt. 1:20-22). The mystery of His virgin birth is a marvelous truth.
2. **His divine life in flesh (vs. 14):** Jesus came to us in flesh. We have seen His grace and glory in His life and ministry. All the divine attributes of God were seen in His life, a perfect and blameless life. He is the true and perfect image of God (Col. 1:15). Before His birth, God had revealed Himself in parts- in His creation and through prophets but in Jesus, it is full and complete. There shall be no such birth and such an event in history anymore.
3. **His resurrection power:** The supreme power of God was demonstrated in raising Jesus from the grave in the likeness of His earthly body. He then appeared to His disciples and several others many times and ascended into heaven to return again. He will receive those who love and trust Him and whose sins have been washed away by the blood that was shed on the cross. The cross was not a defeat but a victory as He rose again.

Jesus is a unique person for He does not belong to history only. Many great people have come and gone in history. Their names have been forgotten or ignored. But can you resist an irresistible person such as Jesus?

Herod ignored His birth and missed Jesus. But the shepherd and wise men met Him and worshipped Him. Meet and see Jesus the Savior of the world during Christmas once again.

Enjoy the gift of joy and peace in Christmas
Luke 2: 1-20

The gift of joy and peace of God came down to earth along with the greatest love gift of God- His only begotten Son

Jesus Christ (John 3:16). The angels declared joy and peace on earth at His birth (Luke 2:10, 14). This joy and peace are divine in nature and permanent in character. These two are inseparable.

It is not peace and joy with one another on Christmas day only. This gift of joy and peace is a fulfilling and everlasting experience. This experience is for those whose sins have been forgiven by the blood of Jesus Christ (1 Peter 1:18-19).

1. **Joy and peace are redemptive:** This joy and peace (rest) are experienced by those who were sinners and are saved and have a right relationship with God. David was restored to enjoy the joy of salvation after he confessed his sin to God (Psalm 51:9-12).
2. **Joy and peace is from the Holy Spirit:** Peace and joy is the fruit of indwelling Holy Spirit (Gal. 5:22). Peace is for those who walk closely with the Lord yielding daily to the leading of the Holy Spirit (Rom. 8:6).
3. **Joy and peace mean service to God:** Jesus said to His disciples, "My peace I give you.... not as the world gives and let not your heart be troubled" (John 14:27). "No one can take away your joy" and "your joy will be complete" (John 16:22,24). Nehemiah had joy in spiritual service and Israel was joyful in building the wall of the temple (Nehemiah 8:10; 12:43).

Jesus promised rest (peace) to those who respond to His invitation to come to Him and accept His Lordship (Matt. 11:28-29). *Your faith in Jesus and joy and peace from Jesus are the cause and effect of Christmas celebration.*

Why Christmas?
John 3: 10-21

Why Son of God became the Son of man is a mystery. The purpose of His coming down to earth in flesh and to live among us unfolds the truth of the mystery. It is ridiculous to celebrate His birth; Christmas without knowing the truth and without recognizing Jesus, the object of the celebration.

1. **The salvation of mankind through Jesus (vs. 15-16):** Christians ought to commemorate the birth of Jesus because through Jesus, God's plan of salvation to free men from guilt and power of sin (Rom. 6:6-7) and to give life eternal was accomplished (Rom. 6:8). This is God's plan since the beginning of creation, when Adam and Eve sinned. Through prophets, God revealed this plan (Isaiah 7:14; Micah 5:2) and fulfilled it, when Jesus the God incarnate was born in Bethlehem (Matt. 1:18-23).

2. **The vicarious death of Jesus on the cross:** The ransom of sin has to be paid; though He had no sin, yet He became sin for us and paid the ransom on the cross of Calvary (2 Cor. 5:21). He carried our sorrows and was crushed for our iniquities (Isaiah 53:5, 7). But He rose again from the grave according to what He had said (Luke 24:6-8). Jesus is alive today (Rev. 1:18).

3. **The glorious return of Jesus (1 Thes. 5:9-10):** It is God's plan for us to live eternally with Him. This is the purpose for which God created man. Jesus will return with might and power, justice and judgment. There shall be separation and selection for those who are righteous in their faith in Christ. Others, shall meet with eternal punishment (Matt. 25: 46).

Therefore, those who are saved have the blessed experience of divine joy and peace in celebrating Christmas.

God became the Son of man so that sons of man will become sons of God.

7.2 New Year

What is your vision this year?
Nehemiah 2: 2-10

God reveals vision to His people for accomplishing His purpose. It is not your desire and purpose to receive vision but it is for accomplishing God's will through His chosen people. It is written, "where there is no vision, the people perish" (Proverbs 29:18 KJV). This means that when you have no self-control, you lack the guidance of the Spirit of God. There is every possibility that you will go astray or get lost.

Therefore, it is time to ask and know God's plan of action in your life, otherwise your resolution for the new year will be in vain.

1. **Vision needs to be revealed (Neh. 1:4):** This calls for human initiative. You need to pray fervently to the mighty and awesome God. There is no revelation to you if you have not surrendered your life fully to the Lord. Without submission, there is no revelation. Nehemiah received a vision for action (Nehemiah 1:11).

2. **Vision is not according to your wish and desire:** God has His own plan for every person and also for every church. It may be a great task or a humble task but any task revealed by God is precious for your response. Obey and honour God's revelation as Nehemiah did (Neh. 3:3)

3. **Vision is accomplished according to God's ways and in His time:** To eliminate human perspective, God allows vision to die for a while. God wants you to learn to wait on Him patiently. He may take you through the valley of death so that you experience the double portion of His grace and realize your inadequacy and inefficiency. God fulfills His plans only in His time (Neh. 2:6-10). He makes everything beautiful in His time (Ecc. 3:12).

Do not, therefore, make a new year resolution and break it. Instead, seek God's grace and receive God's vision for you this year. Expect great things from God and attempt great things for God to make the vision a reality.

Claim God's promises in the New Year
Psalm 34:1-8; 1 Cor. 1:4-9

God told Israel that the year ahead of them would be eventful but the journey would have ups and downs – of mountains and valleys. Nevertheless, God's eyes kept watch over them (Deut. 11: 11-12). The present Israel (believers in Christ) should welcome such promises in the new year without fear and doubt. Even Moses had expressed such fear (Exodus 33:12-13). But God is faithful and His promises are firm (1 Cor. 1:9). When God's presence is with you in your journey, you shall overcome all trials, sufferings and pains that may come in your way. Take refuge in the Lord and you will taste that God is good all the time (Psalm 34:8; Nahum 1:7).

1. **A theological test:** You may be tested about the deity of Jesus Christ, His saving grace and promises. In such situations, stand firm in your faith in Christ to overcome, as were the patriarchs and the prophets (Heb. 11).

2. **A moral test:** As a Christian, you belong to Christ. He is the Saviour and Lord of your life and the outside world will see your life shining in Christ. Let not the world dictate you but may the Word of God be your guide. "One who is in you (Holy Spirit) is greater than the one who is in the world (1 John 4:46).

3. **A social test:** Your love will be visible only when you love the people who are not loved. Jesus Christ, the Master washed the feet of His disciples and asked them to do as He had done to them. When you follow this instruction, the world will know that you are a true disciple of Jesus (John 13:15, 34-35).

"Lord, help me to proclaim Jesus as the Lord ...."

You will be victorious through Him and your identity will not be lost during this year.

Try Christ in the New Year
Matt. 6:25

Do not be afraid or worried of what the new year holds for you (vs. 25, 33-34). His power of resurrection will carry you through the dark hours of life. He alone will be your friend and companion. He is your righteousness and strength, your help and sufficiency (Psalm 23:3-4). Try Christ in faith and in prayer and meditate on His word.

1. **Pray in faith:** Pray in faith believing that He will honor your petition for His name sake (Matt.21: 22). Prayer of a righteousness man is effective (James 4:16b).

2. **Pray for forgiveness of sins:** Pray while confessing your sins. He is faithful and just to forgive and purify all unrighteousness (1 John1:9). Participate in the Holy communion as often as possible to confess sins committed against God and fellow men.

3. **Pray in His glorious name:** When you pray in the glorious name of Jesus Christ, all your needs are met by Him (Phil. 4:19; John 14:13; 16:24). Prayer without honoring His name and without thanksgiving is meaningless and powerless. Let not your words be empty words and repetition of petitions.

4. **Pray continually in praise and thanksgiving (1 Thess. 5:17):** In all circumstances, pray without ceasing giving praise to God. Peace of God will guard your hearts and minds in Christ Jesus (Phil. 4:7).

5. **Meditate on God's Word day and night (Joshua 1:8):** May the Word be a lamp to your feet and light to your path in the new year (Psalm 119:105). If only His Word

and promises are rooted deeply in your heart (Psalm 119:11), you will not fall and sin.

Try Christ in the new year and you will enjoy peace and joy in Christ Jesus throughout the year.

Timelessness of God
Psalm 90

For God, two thousand years have gone by just like a day (vs.4). Apostle Peter reaffirms this truth in 2 Peter 3:8 b- "with the Lord a day is like a thousand years and a thousand years like a day." Christians with unfailing faith in Christ are linked to timeless eternity. The calendar year should make little difference to those who know God truly and deeply and the timelessness of God.

Christians ought to be peaceful and thankful to God when people of this world are worried, and disturbed to welcome the millennium year. The Christians and the church of Christ should welcome the new year with confidence and thanksgiving to God. It is our hope that God will continue to do great and mighty things every year.

1. **God belongs to eternity (vs. 1, 2, 4):** God has created the universe, the sun and the moon. He has no beginning and no end. He does things the way that pleases Him. He can create anything out of nothing. He is absolutely absolute and is above human knowledge and under-standing. He is faithful in all generations from eternity to eternity.

2. **God is above time and space:** Mankind is limited but not God (vs. 10, 12). Every living creature has limited span of life. Every human being has to use time very carefully and profitably for God's glory and for living a fruitful life for himself/herself and the family, church and the society. Do not ignore time. It is precious and time once gone is gone forever.

3. **God planned eternal life:** This is for those who have accepted Jesus Christ as Saviour and Lord of their lives. They have the living hope of eternal life (1 Peter 1 :3-5). Those who have been recreated as a new person in Christ, they enjoy the eternal life on earth and with God in heaven.

May you welcome the millennium in hope and faith in Christ, to make this millennium year a blessed one.

A New Year prayer

Pray without ceasing throughout the new year to overcome the evil designs of devil.

A prayer for all days of the year is " I can do every thing through Him (Christ) who gives me strength" (Phil.4: 13). Continue to pray like:

a. Paul: forgetting things which are behind, pressing forward to reach the goal.
b. Abraham: trust implicitly in God.
c. Enoch: walk in daily fellowship with God.
d. Moses: chose to suffer rather than to enjoy the pleasure of sins for a season.
e. Daniel: commune with God at all times.
f. Job: be patient under all circumstances.
g. Aaron and Hur: uphold the hands of spiritual leaders.
h. Isaiah: consecrate yourself to do God's assigned work.
i. Andrew: lead a brother (a neighbour) to know Christ.
j. Stephen: show forth a forgiving spirit towards all who seek to hurt.
k. Timothy: study the Word of God diligently every day.
l. Israel: lift up your eyes unto the hills and wait for help that comes from God.

God is our hope, who provides and sustain
Psalm 23

In a fast changing world, change takes place quite often. Science and technology change and human beings change in their attitude and values. However, only two things have remained unchanged- God and His divine power and Satan and sin. Trust Jesus who is the same yesterday, today and for ever (Heb. 13:8).

The resurrection of Christ Jesus from the grave is the demonstration of greatest of all powers. Jesus empowers all who are in Him to overcome difficulties and problems that may come your way in the new year. According to the Scripture, "Our God is an ever present help in trouble therefore, we will not fear" (Psalm 46:1). You are also more than conquerors through Jesus Christ who loves us (Rom. 8:37).

Let us not be victims of committing sins but enjoy a victorious life in Christ Jesus.

1. **He provides for all our needs (vs 1):** He is your Jehovah Jireh (Gen. 22: 8 and 14). Therefore, you shall not be in want when God is your shepherd. He meets all your needs through His glorious riches in Christ Jesus (Phil. 4:19).

2. **He sustains us by His presence (vs. 4):** When you cast your cares and anxiety upon Him, He will sustain you (1 Peter 5:7). He will never let the righteous fall if only you have the willing spirit to obey Him. Trust Him and He will lead you throughout the year beside the quiet waters. (vs. 2). He quietens all storms of life. According to His promise "all things God works for the good of those who love Him and have been called according to His purpose" (Romans 8:28).

3. **He is our glorious hope (vs. 6):** He has given you a living hope through the resurrection of Jesus Christ. Jesus Christ

"Lord, help me to proclaim Jesus as the Lord ...."

in you is the hope of glory (Col. 1:27). So, those who are born again long for the glorious eternal life in Christ all the time.

May every morning of the year be a new morning to experience and enjoy His grace and mercy in life (Lam. 3:23). Do not be influenced by the words of the world but by the Word of God.

7.3. Palm Sunday

Paradox of Palm Sunday
Matt. 21: 6-11

The triumphal march of Jesus riding on a donkey and the jubilant crowd that followed Him praising Him all the way to the temple, shouting blessed is the king of Israel, is a paradox. For just after five days, Jesus was carrying the cross to die. This is not a contradiction. This was prophesied many years ago and Jesus had discussed His death on the cross with His disciples and also to the Pharisees. Both the events were according to God's divine plan and became real in His march to the temple at Jerusalem and then to Calvary.

1. **Imperfection in knowing Jesus:** The crowd shouted "Hosanna" meaning "save us now, we pray" and God's plan of salvation through the Messiah was fulfilled (Zech. 9:9). However, the crowd considered Jesus as a prophet (Matt.21: 11). When Jesus saw that they did not understand the prophecy about Him nor did they understand the nature of His kingdom, Jesus wept over Jerusalem (Luke 19:41) because their spiritual eyes were blind.

2. **Inconsistency in following Jesus:** The crowd consisting of Jews, Romans and religious leaders cried, "crucify Him". It was the same crowd that had followed Jesus to the temple. However, when suffering and trial came to

Jesus they went their way. The triumphal march to Jerusalem temple was the shadow of the glorious march of Jesus to Calvary.

Kings of this world live to die but Jesus died to live forever. The kings of this world wear temporal crowns but Jesus wore the crown of thorns of eternal glory. These kings rode on horses and chariots to celebrate victory but Jesus rode on a donkey signifying eternal glory.

You may be excited in following Jesus in the beginning of your walk with Jesus but be careful that you are not inconsistent in your commitments, double minded or self centered while serving God. If so, your relationship is strained and you are not right with God.

Palm Sunday is for purification.

Jesus is the King of the kingdom of God
John 12:12-19; Zech. 9:9

The significance of this day is to recognize Jesus as the king of our lives and not a king according to our convenience, comfort and celebration. It was so with Israel who acknowledged Him as king on Palm Sunday and shouted within a couple of days "crucify Him."

1. **Jesus is the King genealogically:** Jesus came from the tribe of Judah from which the King of Israel came (Luke 1:27 and Matt. 1:17).

2. **Jesus is the King prophetically:** Prophet Zechariah foretold that the Messiah would ride a donkey and not a horse or a chariot and shall be proclaimed as king. The disciples realized this much later when Jesus was glorified and these things happened as they were written (John 12:16)

3. **Jesus is the King theologically:** Jesus is the king of present Israel, figuratively speaking of Jews and Gentiles. Jesus

is the king of those who are sinners and are saved irrespective of their race, colour, caste and nationality (Gal. 3:26-28).

4. **Jesus is the King without a crown:** He wore the crown of thorns for eternal glory. He is not a temporal king of this world. His kingdom spreads all over the world forever and ever.

5. **Jesus is the King without a monarchy:** Jesus rules as the king without monarchy in Christian homes and churches, where democracy and not monarchy is practiced, in perfect harmony and unity in the body of Christ (Romans12: 3-8; 1 Cor.12).

The ministry of the "Stone"
Luke 19:37-44; 1 Peter 2:4-10

When the crowd was shouting "Blessed is the king who comes in the name of the Lord", the Pharisees in the crowd were indignant and asked Jesus to intervene and stop shouting. Jesus quoted from the book of Habakkuk to remind them that if they keep quiet "the stones will cry out" (Habakkuk 2: 11). They were not able to comprehend the meaning of Jesus' triumphal march nor were they able to understand why and how the "stones would cry out".

Jesus established, on this day, very provocatively and deliberately that He is the King of the Kingdom of God. Jesus wept because the spiritual eyes of Israel and Pharisees were blinded and they did not understand the prophecy about Him.

1. **The "living stone" (Jesus) was rejected by men:** Jesus told the Pharisees in the crowd that they had rejected Him thereby they have rejected the truth, justice, love and compassion. They have made unjust gains and have turned the temple, a place of prayer, into a den of robbers (Matt. 21:13). If you are a ritualistic Christian, you are

like a Pharisee, rejecting the living stone, Jesus Christ (1 Peter 2:4).

2. **Be "like living stones" to glorify God (1 Peter 2:5):** Those who shouted, "glory in the highest" even though, they glorified God in their words yet they did not know Jesus personally. It was so with the Pharisees. In riding a donkey in the triumphal march, Jesus was conveying that those who were humble and obedient to His will and purpose, they are like living stones who will cry out His glory and praise (1 Peter 2: 9,10).

Palm Sunday is a day of reflection.

The Lord needs you
Mark 11: 1-10

Palm Sunday is a memorable day for those whose sins are forgiven. This day reminds them of submission and service to Jesus. The Lord needs you for His service in His kingdom.

1. **Untie the bondage of sin to be free:** Jesus said this to signify that His chosen people are often tied to the business of this world so much so that they are not right with Him. They fail to walk with the Lord according to His will and purpose. There are virtues but also vices in their lives (Col. 3:5-10). These sins separate them from God and from the fellowship with believers. Jesus has made provisions to untie you from these stumbling blocks if only you confess your sins and seek forgiveness (1 John 1:9). *Jesus wants you to be free from guilt and power of sin to serve Him.*

2. **Allow Jesus to take charge of your life:** Jesus needs the colt which no one has ridden (vs.2) is now untied for use by Jesus. If you are not cleansed by His blood, you are not needed to serve His purpose. Jesus needs you to serve Him if only you are redeemed and sins do not have any

dominion over you (Romans 8:1). You have to take off your cloak of unrighteousness and lay them at His feet signifying your full and glad surrender.

3. **Accepts Jesus as your Master:** Jesus rode on the colt of a donkey that was humble and obedient. He did not use a strong and stout charger, a horse because His kingdom does not belong to this world.

If you want to celebrate Palm Sunday in praising and singing "Hosanna to the highest", you ought to be humble and obey His commandments.

7.4 Good Friday

Seven remarkable words of Christ from the cross

Christ spoke these words when he was nailed to the cross and before he died.

1. **Luke 23:34:** "Father, forgive them." "Them" include all those who shall repent and believe the gospel including His enemies who were nailing Him to the cross. This "forgiveness" that Jesus was asking for the enemies is not similar to pardoning or excusing someone for disobedience or mistake. Even when Jesus was suffering from unrecoverable damage into death, He is pleading with the Father advocating on behalf of His enemies for the forgiveness of their sin. "For they do not know what they were doing." He was thus reconciling the sinless God with sinful men. Realise that forgiveness of sin is only at the cross of Calvary, where Jesus paid the price for the remission of sin.

   Christ set an example of what He had preached – "Love your enemies."

2. **Luke 23:43:** This is the response of Jesus to the prayer of a dying sinner to a dying Savior. One criminal hanging on the cross challenged Jesus to meet his physical need to release him from the cross; whereas the other criminal was confessing and repenting for his sin and was showing his faith in Jesus Christ. This criminal's need was spiritual, for he asked Jesus to remember him in His Kingdom.

   Jesus suffered and died on the cross not only to purchase forgiveness for our sins but also to purchase eternal life for all those who trust Him as their personal Savior and Lord of their lives.

3. **John 19:26-27:** Jesus address His mother "Woman". Jesus paid with His life on the cross to secure justification for all men and women. Jesus had a divine purpose to accomplish on the cross and earthly connections had lost their purpose and meaning. But He was conscious of the wounded heart of His mother gazing at Him hanging on the cross. Jesus made provision for her by entrusting her to one of His disciples. It is an example of divine goodness. Jesus expects from you similar social responsibilities to honour.

4. **Mark 15:34; Matthew 27:46:** Jesus was in agony when He cried out, "My God, my God, why have you forsaken me ?" It is a strange prayer from Jesus as He was in extreme pain and anguish because He was hanging on the cross for six hours in the hot sun.

   Above all, it was so hard for Him, who knew no sin to be made sin for us and to bear punishment of death on the cross for all of us (2 Cor. 5:21; Romans 5:6-8).

   Paying the ransom for sin, Christ being forsaken by His Father, was the most grievous of His sufferings. But this momentary separation from His father was hard for Him to take.

But Jesus through this momentary separation opened up a permanent way to the salvation for sinful men to eternal life in heaven and on earth, once and for all.

5. **John 19:28, 30**: Jesus cried, "I thirst" and thereafter said, "It is finished."

Physically and emotionally, He was thirsty because of the agony of His death. He was physically weak and emotionally charged to call for water to quench His thirst; but He was given vinegar instead. When heaven denied Him a beam of light, earth deprived Him a drop of water.

"It is finished" signifies that He had completed and finished the task socially, politically and religiously. He had compassion for those who were hungry. He fed them. He did miracle to heal those who were sick. Politically, he taught the Scripture to Pharisees and teachers of law. In obeying and honoring the law, Jesus gave meaning to religious life. He had finished the work of salvation. He did not leave anything unfinished in God's plan of salvation for mankind. He destroyed and conquered death for those who believe in Him. He alone can say, "It is finished." It is significant because no man can claim that He has finished everything.

6. **Luke 23:46:** Jesus said, "I submit to you, (deposit with you) my Father, my mental, emotional and physical self." To whom can the Spirit of men be submitted ? Only to the creator of body, mind and soul.

He now returns to the Father for reunion with Him. Jesus returns triumphantly and gloriously to His Father.

The message of the cross

Dying on a cross was the most shameful and degrading experience. Crucifixion was the cruelest punishment meant for worst kind of criminals. The Scripture tells us, "Cursed is every one who hangs on a tree" (Deut. 21:23; Gal 3:13). This hopeless and helpless situation had become the ground of our justification and hope of eternal life. Thus, cross is the glory of all those who have been redeemed by the blood shed on Calvary's cross. Apostle Paul writes, "But God forbid that I should glory except in the cross of our Lord Jesus Christ" (Gal 6:14).

1. **Love and justice met on the cross :** For a natural man, it is difficult to understand this mystery. Jesus sacrificed Himself on the cross to reconcile the love and justice of the holy God and sinful men. Because of God's love, His Son bore upon Himself the sorrow and the pain and paid the penalty for sin on the cross to set men free from the bondage of sin.

   God loved us first (1 John 4:19) so much so that He gave His one and the only Son Jesus Christ to us that whoever believed in Him would not die but shall have eternal life. "God demonstrates His own love towards us in that while we were sinners, Christ died for us" (Rom. 5:8). As we want to experience, His love, we must recognise first the gravity of sin. This is so serious that it can not be ignored by the holy and just God. Since there is no remission of sin without shedding of blood (Heb. 9:22), reconciliation of just God and sinful men is only possible through Jesus Christ who shed His blood without blemish on the cross.

2. **Cross is the glory of God :** Jesus looked beyond the pain and suffering on the cross to future glory. In Heb. 12:2, it is written "Who for the joy set before Him endured the cross scorning its shame and set down at the right hand of the throne of God. "Apostle Paul reminds the church at Philippi (Phil. 2:8-11)." And made in the appearance of a man, He humbled Himself and became obedient to death on the cross. Therefore, God exalted Him to the highest place and gave Him the name that is above every name

that at the name of Jesus every knee should bow in heaven and under the earth and every tongue confess that Jesus Christ is Lord to the glory of God, the Father."

Cross is not the final word in the gospel. It is His resurrection from the grave. Likewise, suffering and pain is not final but an essential step to glorify God. Therefore, followers of Jesus are not exempted from suffering and pain but when the glory is revealed, they will be overjoyed (1 Peter 4:13f). Early Christians considered it a blessing to suffer for Christ (Phil. 1:29).

3. **Reward of the cross :** This reward is of priceless value. It is the glory of God in you. For this purpose, Christians are recreated, born anew in Christ to share the glory of God.

"Jesus Christ laid down His life for us, and we ought to lay down our lives for our brothers" (1 John 3:16). Are you ready to lay down your life for Christ ? Apostle Paul wrote "I have been crucified with Christ, I no longer live but Christ lives in me. The life I lead in the body, I live by faith in the son of God" (Gal. 2:20).

Early church was a persecuted church as they waited for the priceless reward in heaven. In all circumstances, suffering and trial of faith, cross is the refuge, help and strength. Jesus exhorted His disciples giving His own example. "In this world, you will have trouble, but take heart, I have overcome the world" (John 16:33). Apostle Peter in 1 Pet. 1:5-7 encourages the Christians in Asia Minor. "In this you greatly rejoice though now for little while you may have had suffered grief in all kinds of trials ... may result in glory and honour whom Jesus Christ is revealed." This is the glorious reward for each follower of Christ.

Cross is the pivotal point of the church of Christ. Cross stands uniquely at the top of the church to declare the glory of God.

7.5 *Easter*

"Where O death is your victory?"
John 20:10-18; 1 Cor. 15: 50-58

Tragedy of Good Friday became triumph on resurrection day (Sunday). Without the resurrection of Christ, the cross would have gone down in history as an insignificant event. The redemptive act of Christ on the cross would have lost the meaning and God's plan of salvation would have been frustrated without resurrection. Resurrection of Christ brought three-fold victory for all who are in Christ.

1. **Victory in the new-life in Christ :** New life in Christ brought new responsibilities to proclaim Christ's death and resurrection with conviction (Acts 4:20). The disciples had a victorious life in the midst of persecution, trials and sufferings.

   Mary was the first one to be commissioned to go and to tell that Christ is risen and He is alive (John 20:18). Are you sharing Christ's death and resurrection with others? (1 Cor. 15:58) "Your labour in the Lord is not in vain."

2. **Victory in the resurrected power of Jesus :** It is the power of the Holy Spirit which the disciples received after the resurrection and ascension of Jesus Christ. They were emboldened to live a victorious life to win souls for Christ. It is written that the handful disciples "turned the world uphold down" (Acts 17.6 KJV).

3. **Victory in the resurrection of believers in Christ (vs. 50-54):** Mortality gives place to immortality in the resurrection of those who die in Christ. It is victory for

them who rise from the grave imperishable. Death has been swallowed up in victory.

God grants you this victory today through our Lord Jesus Christ.

A new beginning in history
Luke 24:1-12; 1 Cor. 15:1-11

Resurrection of Jesus is a sovereign act and therefore has a purpose. His passion and death were not in themselves an end of God's plan for eternal life (salvation) of men.

1. **The history of the Easter day:** The news of the empty tomb (Luke 24:5) was unacceptable to the disciples. Rather, they were perplexed and puzzled, forgetting what Jesus had told them about His death and that He would rise from the grave on the third day. They had forgotten this (Luke 24:11). It was unbelievable in the beginning of the day but during the day Jesus proved that He was alive by appearing to His disciples. He appeared several times to the disciples and also to more than five hundred people (1 Cor. 15:4-5). Do you dismiss this truth on flimsy grounds?

2. **The turning point in history after Easter:** The angel in the empty tomb said to the disciples, "Come and see: Go and tell" (Matt. 28: 6, 8). It is an invitation to us to see and know the power of resurrection of Christ and to realise the importance of the mystery of Christ's death and resurrection. So we have to go and tell this to the unbelieving world with conviction. Tell the people that Christ is risen and alive for ever.

Resurrection is the victory of righteousness of God over evil. *It is the victory of love, truth and justice over hatred, falsehood and corruption.*

Resurrection - A fact of human experience
John 20:1-8

Christian faith stands on the historical facts of resurrection and of human experience. The enemies of Christ tried to disapprove the fact of resurrection but could not succeed for three objective truths.

1. **The resurrection of Jesus brought about a new man with new dignity (2 Cor. 5:17):** The gospel brought salvation to the soul and dignity to men, women and even children (Eph 1:10). Our personal salvation is founded on the reality of the resurrection of Christ.

2. **The resurrection of Jesus brought about a new man in a new society (Eph. 2:15, 16, 19):** Christ broke down all barriers in human society and brought about brotherhood through His love and goodness for men. Acceptance of Onesimus (Philemon Verse 10) not only tells us what is right but also tells us to do what is right (Rom. 6:4).

3. **The resurrection of Jesus brought about a new man with new hope (Acts 1:10):** Human race lives in fear of death. There is the concept of one life and one death and then comes judgment. Resurrection of Jesus Christ brought hope of resurrection to all who believe in Him. It is hope with expectation beyond death for Christ has defeated death by rising from the grave on the third day.

Life with resurrected Christ is endless hope and life without Christ is a hopeless end.

7.6 Harvest thanksgiving

Thanksgiving is offering sacrifices to God
Lev. 23 : 9-12; Deut 26:10-11; Heb. 13:15-16

Harvest thanksgiving is celebrated year after year by offering the harvest of the good earth. The Israelites celebrated the harvest thanksgiving to fulfill the law (Deut. 26: 10,11).

We, the present Israel should celebrate the festival of the harvest of thanksgiving by offering the harvest of souls to God.

1. **Thanksgiving is to offer the sacrifice of living body to God:** Our offering is symbolic to God, for God offered His son Jesus Christ for us. In response, we offer to God living sacrifice of our living body to Him (Rom. 12:1). We can offer the harvest of souls in response to His greatest gift of His Son Jesus for our salvation and eternal life.
2. **Thanksgiving is offering in faith:** When sacrifices become ritual, God said to Israel, "Your sacrifices do not please me" (Jer. 6:20). God accepted the offering of Abel whose sacrifice was a better sacrifice than Cain's (Heb. 11:4). Cain's thanksgiving was a ritualistic celebration but Abel's thanks offering was in faith.
3. **Thanksgiving is to offer sacrifice of praise and worship (Heb. 13:15):** It is the fruit of the Spirit and love of God that compels us to praise and worship Him. Offering our living body as living sacrifice to Him is a spiritual act of worship (Rom. 12:1).

7.7 Wedding

The truth of Christian wedding
Gen. 2:20-24; Eph. 5:22-32

The scriptural teachings are not for couples getting married but are useful to all married couples, eligible bachelors and spinsters present in the wedding service.

1. **It is theocentric (God centred):** God is the Originator and Architect of marriage. It is not Adam but God who originated marriage (Gen. 2:21). Christian wedding is solemnised in the presence of God in the sanctuary. It is a sacred institution established by God. When wedding becomes personal and private, it is not under the blessing

of God and such weddings are likely to break down. "Every thing God does will endure forever" (Eccl. 3:14b).

2. **It is a profound mystery (Eph. 5:32):** In creation, God made two bodies out of one body and in wedding two bodies become one body. When the couples minds are transformed, their attitude and emotions adjust and confirm to a love relationship, which will grow deeper and stronger with time.

   Jesus did transform water into wine in a wedding in Cana but now we pray that He will transform the minds of the couple. This miracle transcends inadequacies, disagreements, anger and anxieties of the couple.

3. **Wives submit to husbands and husbands love your wives (Eph. 5:22-29):** The submission is not subordination or subjugation; it is a disposition– willing to yield to respect the husband. Such wives are noble and husband's crown (Prov. 12:4).

   The husband's love for his wife is unselfish, sacrificial and divine. The husband protects, helps and honours her in all situations. Such a husband receives favour from God (Pro 18:22).

4. **A couple who prays and worships together, stays together**: It is not important how the couple start their married life but how they finish is important. They are united into Christ in prayer and worship.

Christian marriage is a relationship with God
Matt. 19:1-9

A couple's relationship with God is a fulfilling experience to cherish. The couple ought to strive to maintain the relationship with God till death separate.

   1. An unique relationship: Wedding is not performed but solemnised in God's presence. The couple commit to each other by taking vows. The Bible says, the relationship is divine and ordained by God (Gen. 2:22).

2. An intimate relationship (Matt. 19:5,6): The intimacy is in one body. Husband and wife are no longer two but one organism. Even though they are two different personalities; yet they operate as one in mind and spirit. "Do not be yoked together with an unbeliever." If so, the couple will find it hard to contain their marriage.

3. An exclusive relationship (Math 19:5): Both have to leave something that belonged to them to cleave to each other. This does not mean to disdain parents but emphasise on being loyal to the life partner above everything.

4. A purposeful relationship: The couple share their body, mind and spirit with each other. They live together to propagate human race (Gen. 1:28).

5. An imperfect relationship: Marriage which is based on feelings and emotions breakdown. When the couple looks for the thrill of their first love through out their married life, they are disillusioned. Each partner ought to die to themselves several times to make their imperfections perfect. It is not by adjustments alone but by forgiveness and love towards each other, the couple enjoy a glorious and a blessed life.

ABOUT THE AUTHOR:

Mohit Kumar Pramanik had a brilliant academic career in engineering and management studies in India and abroad. A gold medalist of Utkal University in Physics, he went to study engineering at the IISc, Bangalore and thereafter to the Carnegic Institute of Technology, Pittsburgh, USA to study post graduate engineering in steel technology.

After his return, he joined SAIL in 1962 and while in SAIL, he went on deputation to Ministry of Steel and Mines as the Industrial Advisor to Government of India for five years. He specialised in management studies at IIM, Calcutta, Administrative Staff College of India, Hyderabad and finally at the London Management College, Henley-on Thames, UK.

In his three decades in secular and professional services, he diligently upheld the values of honesty and integrity. In response to the Lord's call to join the Circular Road Baptist Chapel as its pastor, he resigned the office of Managing Director (Marketing) in 1991.

The commitment he and his wife had to save the soul through pastoral ministry and their love for the congregation had endeared them to one and all who came to know them. During his pastoral ministry, he and his wife spearheaded the vision of establishing a sister church for Bengali speaking new converts in south Calcutta before his retirement.

He was closely associated with several Christian organisations - the UESI and EFI and is currently associated with the Serampore College Council, the Board of Theological Education of the Senate and World Vision, India.

He has attended several evangelical conferences including the conferences organised by the Billy Graham Evangelistic Association in Singapore in 1968 and in Lausanne, Switzerland in 1974. As a Baptist leader, he attended the Asian Baptist

Churches Federation Conference at Singapore in 1993 and the Baptist World Alliance Conference at Buenos Aires, Argentina in 1996.

After he took retirement, he accepted the title of Doctor of Divinity (Honoris Causa) from the Trans-World Ministries, USA and another from the Academy of Ecumenical Theology and Church Administration, Chennai, India.

He and his wife come from Orissa but they now live in Delhi. But they may be soon moving to settle down in their home in Bangalore.

They are blessed with two daughters and three lovely grand children - Ruth Shilpanjali, Rebecca Nilanjana and Daniel Nishant.

www.ingramcontent.com/pod-product-compliance
Lightning Source LLC
Chambersburg PA
CBHW022132080426
42734CB00006B/337